Northumbria
and
Hadrian's Wall

AA Publishing

Author: David Winpenny
Page layout: Jo Tapper

Reprinted 2004,
3rd edition 2002.
Produced by AA Publishing
© Automobile Association
Developments Limited 2004.
Original edition printed 1996.

Published by AA Publishing
(a trading name of Automobile
Association Developments Limited,
whose registered office is
Millstream, Maidenhead Road,
Windsor, Berkshire, SL4 5GD.
Registered Number 1878835)

 Ordnance
Survey® This product
includes
mapping data licensed from
Ordnance Survey® with the
permission of the Controller of Her
Majesty's Stationery Office.
© Crown copyright 2004. All rights
reserved. Licence number 399221

Mapping produced by the
Cartographic Department of The
Automobile Association. A02133.

ISBN 07495 3297 1

A CIP catalogue record for this
book is available from the British
Library.

Gazetteer map references are taken
from the National Grid and can be
used in conjunction with Ordnance
Survey maps and atlases. Places
featured in this guide will not
necessarily be found on the maps
at the back of the book.

All the walks are on rights of way,
permissive paths or on routes
where de facto access for walkers is
accepted. On routes which are not
on legal rights of way, but where
access for walkers is allowed by
local agreements, no implication of
a right of way is intended.

Visit the AA Publishing website at
www.theAA.com

Colour reproduction by L C Repro

Printed and bound by G. Canale &
C. s.p.a., Torino, Italy

Contents

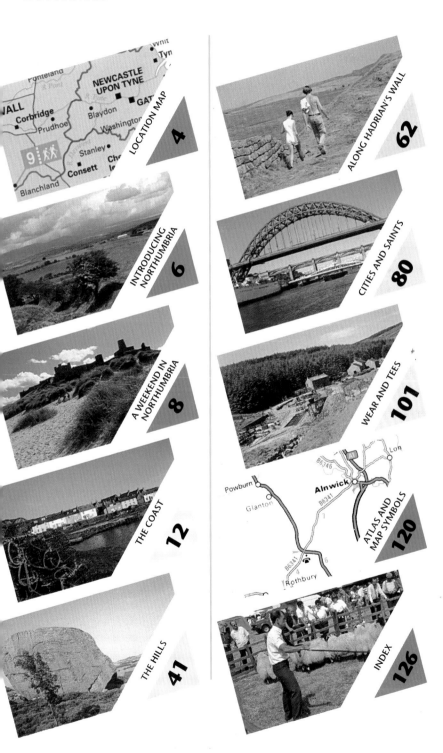

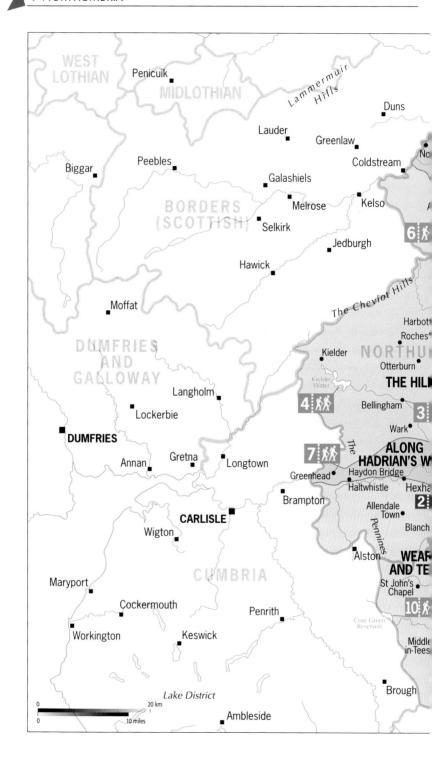

WEST
LOTHIAN

MIDLOTHIAN

Penicuik

Lammermuir Hills

Duns

Lauder

Greenlaw

Coldstream

No

Biggar

Peebles

Galashiels

Melrose

Kelso

6

Selkirk

BORDERS
(SCOTTISH)

Jedburgh

Hawick

The Cheviot Hills

Moffat

Harbot

Roches

Kielder

NORTHU

DUMFRIES
AND
GALLOWAY

Otterburn

THE HIL

Kielder
Water

4

Bellingham

3

Langholm

Wark

Lockerbie

7

ALONG
HADRIAN'S W

DUMFRIES

Gretna

Longtown

The

Greenhead

Haydon Bridge

Annan

Haltwhistle

Hexha

Brampton

2

Allendale
Town

CARLISLE

Blanch

Wigton

Pennines

Alston

WEAR
AND TE

CUMBRIA

St John's
Chapel

Maryport

10

Cockermouth

Penrith

Cow Green
Reservoir

Workington

Keswick

Middle
in-Tees

0   20 km

0   10 miles

Lake District

Brough

Ambleside

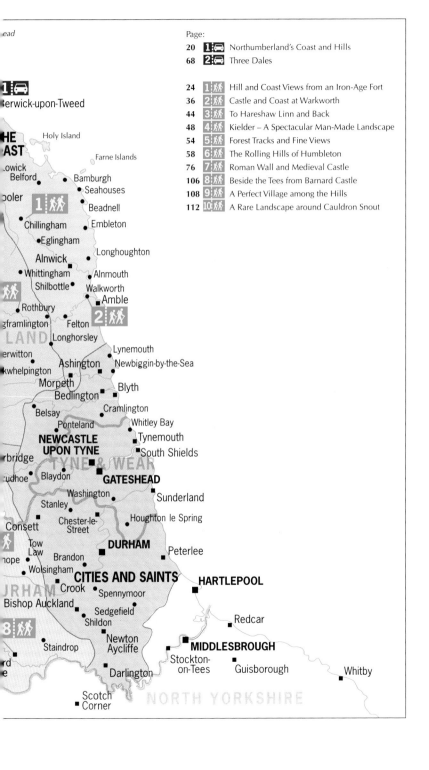

ead

1 🚗
erwick-upon-Tweed

**HE
AST**

Holy Island

Farne Islands

owick
Belford
ooler
Chillingham
Eglingham
Alnwick
Whittingham
Shilbottle
Rothbury
gframlington
erwitton
kwhelpington
Morpeth
Bedlington
Belsay
Ponteland
**NEWCASTLE
UPON TYNE**
rbridge
udhoe   Blaydon
Stanley
Consett
Tow
Law
hope   Brandon
Wolsingham
CITIES AND SAINTS
Crook
Bishop Auckland
8 🚶
Staindrop
rd
e

Bamburgh
Seahouses
Beadnell
Embleton
Longhoughton
Alnmouth
Walkworth
Amble
2 🚶
Felton
Longhorsley
Lynemouth
Newbiggin-by-the-Sea
Blyth
Cramlington
Whitley Bay
Tynemouth
South Shields
GATESHEAD
Washington
Sunderland
Houghton le Spring
Chester-le-
Street
DURHAM
Peterlee
Spennymoor
Sedgefield
Shildon
Newton
Aycliffe
Darlington

1 🚶

🚶

LAND

Ashington

TYNE & WEAR

Scotch
Corner

HARTLEPOOL

Redcar

MIDDLESBROUGH
Stockton-
on-Tees   Guisborough   Whitby

JRHAM

NORTH YORKSHIRE

Introducing Northumbria

Northumbria is a vast swathe of northeast England, from the fiercely contested Scottish Border to the boundary of Yorkshire; from the High Pennines – England's last wilderness – to the golden sands along Northumberland's coast. It encompasses the smooth Cheviot Hills and the rugged Simonsides, deep river valleys, expansive Kielder Water and huge tracts of forest, as well as vibrant Newcastle upon Tyne, historic Durham, the secret valleys of the Tees and Wear, and the fascinating industrial history of the Tyne.

The borderlands were fought over for centuries: Stone-Age and Iron-Age men dug hilltop forts; Hadrian constructed his Wall to control entry to his Empire; the great lords of the Middle Ages built their castles as protection from Scottish raiders. And, in the midst of this fighting, great saints ministered – St Aidan, St Cuthbert, and St Godric among them – and The Venerable Bede wrote his *Ecclesiastical History*. Inventors, too, had their home here, including George Stephenson and Lord Armstrong. Northumbria's heroine, Grace Darling, lived her short life on – and off – the coast, and native artistic life is represented by Thomas Bewick and Catherine Cookson.

WALKING
Below, Northumbria's unspoiled, wide open spaces offer great opportunities for walking and other activities

DIRTY BOTTLES
Northumbria is a land rich in legend and superstition – none stranger than that of Alnwick's 'Dirty Bottles' pub, above

CAUSEY ARCH
Left, this venerable bridge near Beamish marks a high point of 18th-century railway engineering

GRACE DARLING
The brave young woman who rowed out in a storm to help the victims of a shipwreck off the Farne Islands is justly celebrated in Bamburgh

TICKLE THE PALATE
Look out for delicacies such as the richly smoked Craster kippers and the local Cotherstone cheese, left

CAULDRON SNOUT
The cascade of Cauldron Snout in Upper Teesdale, right, is one of a number of spectacular waterfalls in the region

FLORA
Upper Teesdale supports a unique and very special flora, including the rare Teesdale violet, below

HADRIAN'S WALL
Much of the 73-mile (117.5-km) length of this great structure can still be traced today, a sturdy tribute to its 2nd-century builders

THE ESSENTIAL NORTHUMBRIA
If you have little time and want to sample the essence of Northumbria:

View the Cheviot Hills, the beautiful coast, including Holy Island, and several castles from Ros Castle...**Visit** Alnwick Castle, fortress home of the Dukes of Northumberland, with its fairy-tale interiors...**Walk** down Grey Street in Newcastle – one of the most elegant in Europe – and on to view the famous Tyne bridges...**Explore** Housesteads Roman Fort (not on a Bank Holiday or fine summer weekend, though!), or walk at Walltown... **Drive** from St John's Chapel over Harthope Moor – spectacular moorland scenery – and down to High Force waterfall... **See** St Cuthbert' shrine in magnificent Durham Cathedral... **Sample** a Singin' Hinnie – a girdle cake with currants – or a pair of traditionally smoked Craster kippers.

THOMAS BEWICK
Right, the great illustrator and engraver Thomas Bewick was a Northumberland man, born in Cherryburn in 1753

ST CUTHBERT
The well-loved Northumbrian saint is associated with a rocky cave in Glendale, left, near the village of Doddington

NORTHUMBRIA'S TEN BEST CASTLES
Alnwick
Bamburgh
Barnard
Chillingham
Dunstanburgh
Durham
Lindisfarne
Newcastle
Raby
Warkworth

RABY CASTLE
The magnificent, moated castle of Raby is one of many in this richly fortified region

WALLING
While not on a scale comparable with Roman construction, building and repairing of walls, left, is a skill still practised in Northumbria today

CATHEDRAL CITY
Lovely Durham's winding streets offer secret corners and ancient devices amidst the city stonework, right

HOSPITALE EPI DUNELM
PRO VIII PAUPERIBUS
FUNDAT PER JOH EPISCOP
A·D·MDCLXVI

A Weekend in Northumbria: Day One

Ideally, Northumbria should be taken slowly, like a good wine, but if you can only manage a weekend, these pages suggest a loosely-planned intinerary. It will take you to a few of the highlights of this huge area, which extends to more than 3,000 square miles.

There are options for wet weather, and suggestions of places that will interest children, where possible. Places in the Gazetteer are in **bold**.

Friday Night

Stay in or around **Bamburgh** – Waren House, 3 miles (4.8km) west is a fine Georgian house in wooded grounds overlooking Budle Bay. If you prefer the village inn type of accommodation, the Blue Bell Hotel at Belford is highly recommended. Take an evening stroll around Bamburgh to view its magnificent medieval castle in the fading light and look for Grace Darling's grave in the churchyard.

Treat yourself to a night of warm hospitality at the Blue Bell Hotel in Belford, above

Saturday Morning

Drive from Bamburgh along the coast road to **Seahouses** and take a boat trip from the busy harbour around the **Farne Islands** – fascinating for children and adults. There are reminders of the Dark Ages saints here, but most visitors come to view the wildlife, including seals and sea-birds – puffins, fulmars, petrels, terns, kittiwakes, guillemots, oyster-catchers and cormorants. Don't forget your hat, and preferably wear old clothes – the birds don't try to miss!

For bird and sea life, head out to the fascinating Farne Islands, left

Right, enjoy a good lunch at the Ship Inn, in Seahouses, and walk it off again in the Cheviots, below

Saturday Lunch

Back on dry land, lunch calls. Among the variety of good eating places in Seahouses, the Olde Ship Hotel, with its nautical memorabilia, can be recommended. There is a lounge where children are welcome, and a small garden.

Saturday Afternoon

Drive south to Beadnell and then head inland, cross the A1 near North Charlton and take the minor road over the hills to Ros Castle. If the weather is clear, why not take the Ros Castle Walk (see page 24) for stunning views of the coast and the Cheviot Hills.

After your walk, drive south through Old Bewick and on to the B6346 through Eglingham into **Alnwick**. The castle is wonderful inside and out – or you can just enjoy the craft shops and bustle of this lively town.

When in Alnwick, don't miss Alnwick Castle, right

From Alnwick take the B6341 south west through Edlingham to the A697. Turn south towards Newcastle.

Saturday Night

Pamper yourself at Linden Hall Hotel, below

If your budget will stretch to it, treat yourself to a night at the Linden Hall Hotel, just north of Longhorsley on the A697. Set in 450 acres of fine grounds, it is a luxurious country house with a porticoed entrance and a grand inner hall. It has a first-class restaurant, a lively pub-restaurant in the old stables and an enormous range of sport and leisure activities, including a swimming pool. **Morpeth**, 6 miles (9.6km) south, offers plenty of alternatives.

A Weekend in Northumbria: Day Two

The second of our two-day visit to Northumbria offers a great house, castle and garden, Roman antiquities on Hadrian's Wall, and a visit to the exciting city of Durham.

Sunday Morning

Drive to Morpeth centre, then take the B6524 through Edlington and Whalton (where, at dusk on 4 July, villagers follow an old tradition and light a great bonfire – the Baal Fire – on the village green) to **Belsay**, with its unusual 19th-century Greek-style house, 14th-century castle and picturesque garden.

Then drive up the A696 towards Otterburn for 5 miles (8km), turn left on the B6342, cross the A68 and take the A6079 through Chollerton. Then go right to join the B6318, which runs beside (and sometimes on top of) Hadrian's Wall. Follow signs for **Chesters** fort – with one of the best-preserved Roman bath houses on the Wall.

If it's wet, go straight to Hexham.

Take in medieval Belsay Castle, above

Step back to Roman times at Chesters fort, left

Discover the delights of historic Hexham, below

Sunday Lunch

Back to the A6079 and into **Hexham** for lunch. There is plenty of choice in and around the town, but one good place is The Rat at Anick, just north-east of the roundabout on the A69, which offers a traditional Sunday lunch with plenty of choice. Children are welcome and there is a pleasant garden, but no animals are allowed, except guide dogs.

Sunday Afternoon

After lunch, leave Hexham on the B6306 over the hills to see the perfect village of **Blanchland**, a cluster of stone houses built for lead miners in the mid-18th century and beautifully preserved by the Trustees who own the estate.

Continue beside the Derwent Reservoir to Edmundbyers, where you join the B6278 to Consett, and eventually the A691 into **Durham.**

For rural delights, leave time to explore Blanchland, top, and enjoy tranquil Derwent Reservoir, above

Finish with a walk around the highlights of the lovely old city of Durham, right and below

An official World Heritage Site, Durham has a spectacular setting high above a loop of the River Wear. At its heart are the magnificent cathedral and the nearby castle, which is now used by the university, and there are delightful old streets to explore and museums and galleries to visit.

A good introduction to the city would be to follow our Walk around Durham (see page 87), which takes in the old town, the cathedral and the castle.

The Coast

From historic Berwick-upon-Tweed to Druridge Bay, the golden Northumberland coast sweeps south, with a chain of strong castles: Alnwick, home of the powerful Percy family; Bamburgh, with its wholly medieval appearance; Chillingham, which had a particularly turbulent history; the dramatic ruins of Dunstanburgh; Warkworth, known by Shakespeare. Holy Island and the Farne Islands were the heartland of the Dark-Age northern saints, St Aidan and St Cuthbert, who kept alive Christianity. Amidst all this history there are nature reserves and bird-sheltering rocks, quiet country roads winding through gentle hills, and a wonderful sense of freedom under a spacious northern sky.

ALNMOUTH Northumberland Map ref NU2410

Alnmouth glitters like a jewel beside the estuary of the River Aln. Houses cluster on the spur of land and round the harbour, home to pleasure craft, and good sandy beaches line the coast. It is a quiet town, a good holiday centre and, with two golf courses, popular with sports-lovers.

The village of Alnmouth is blessed with sandy beaches and a safe harbour

Alnmouth was a planned village and the main sea port for Alnwick in medieval times, and was busy

handling corn in the 18th century. Some of the tall granaries, with their small windows, have been converted into houses – the Marine House Hotel is one of them.

When John Wesley visited in 1748 he damned Alnmouth as famous for all types of wickedness, so it may have been divine retribution when a storm on Christmas Day 1806 changed the course of the river. It cut off the ruins of the Norman Church of St Waleric which was on the conical Church Hill across the harbour – a single cross now marks the site – and led to the slow silting up of the harbour, which struggled on until the 1880s before the town became the peaceful holiday centre it is today.

ALNWICK   Northumberland Map ref NU1813

Alnwick (pronounced 'Annick') has been the stronghold of the powerful Percy family, who became the Dukes of Northumberland, since 1309. Alnwick Castle's strong walls and round towers, although altered over the centuries, owe their outline to the Normans. Its barbican – the best surviving in Britain – and the impressive gateway, with stone figures mimicking an ever-watchful garrison, were added when the Percys arrived.

The medieval interiors were transformed into a Renaissance palace by the 4th Duke in the 19th century.

A SMALL PLACE IN NAVAL HISTORY
In 1779 Alnmouth was fired on from the sea by the *Ranger,* an American ship fighting for the French and commanded by the former pirate, John Paul Jones. He aimed at the church but the cannonball missed by several hundred yards and hit a farmhouse.

MEDIEVAL FUN
Visit Alnwick at the end of June to get a taste of medieval life at Alnwick Fair Week. It begins with a costumed street procession on the last Sunday in the month, when there is outdoor entertainment and craft stalls, as well as an ox-roast. Festivities continue throughout the week, with people in medieval garb mingling with the visitors. There is even a ducking stool for young women led astray during the fun! Alnwick also hosts an International Music Festival in August, with musicians and dancers from all over Europe.

Join in the fun of Alnwick's 'medieval' fair

From the bridge the view of Alnwick Castle clearly shows the stone figures standing high on the battlements, placed there to intimidate would-be attackers

SHIPS AND BOTTLES

While you are in Alnwick, don't miss the Olympic Room at the White Swan Hotel, with woodwork and fittings salvaged from the *Olympic*, the sister ship of the *Titanic*, and the Old Cross Inn, which is known as the 'Dirty Bottles'. This Narrowgate hostelry has a display of old bottles in its window which have remained untouched for more than 150 years, since a former landlord died while trying to rearrange them. Superstitious fears of a death curse have prevented any of his successors from attempting to do the same.

It glows with fine woodwork and marble and is filled with treasures, including paintings by Canaletto, Titian, Van Dyck and Andrea del Sarto. There are two stunning cabinets made for Louis XIV, and two great Meissen dinner services.

The castle parkland was landscaped by 'Capability' Brown, a Northumberland man (see page 53). It is dotted with romantic buildings, mostly constructed for the 1st Duke, including the Brizlee Tower, six storeys of folly by Robert Adam. His brother John designed the Lion Bridge with its cast lead Percy lion.

The castle does not dominate the attractive stone-built town, but its influence is apparent. The 15th-century parish church lies near the castle, while at the other end of town is a survivor of the town walls begun in 1434, the narrow Hotspur Gate, named after the most famous of the Percys, Shakespeare's Harry Hotspur. From the park gate you can walk to the gateway to Alnwick Abbey and continue beyond that to peaceful Hulne Priory, further up the valley.

Alnwick's cobbled market place bustles with life, and there are plenty of shops selling local produce, crafts and antiques. The former railway station houses one of Britain's largest second-hand book shops. Opposite the station is a column which was erected by grateful farmers when the 3rd Duke lowered their rents. The 4th Duke raised them again, and the column subsequently became known as Farmers' Folly.

The Pastures below the castle is the scene for a mammoth Shrove Tuesday football match, which uses the Lion and Denwick Bridges as goals. The match is played between the people of the parish of St Michael and the people of the parish of St Paul.

AMBLE Northumberland Map ref NU2604
Amble, at the mouth of the River Coquet, owes its
existence to coal. There are fragments of a medieval
manor in the High Street, but Amble remained a hamlet
until the 1840s, when the harbour was built to export
coal from the Northumbrian coalfield. This trade came
to an end in 1969, since when Amble has developed as a
holiday town. Its impressive marina has moorings for
200 boats and a public slipway, and boat trips leave the
harbour for Coquet Island (see Walk on page 36).

To the south of the town, the Northumberland
Wildlife Trust runs Hauxley Nature Reserve, with hides
for bird-watching, but you will need a permit from the
information centre. Northumberland County Council's
Druridge Bay Country Park has a visitor centre and
pleasant walks beside Ladyburn Lake. The great sweep of
Druridge Bay itself, owned in part by the National Trust,
offers miles of golden sand dunes and grassland. Just
inland, near Widdrington, are the ruins of Chibburn
Preceptory, a small medieval house and chapel of the
Knights Hospitaller, first recorded in 1313.

BAMBURGH Northumberland Map ref NU1734
Bamburgh for most visitors means the castle,
dominating both the village and the coast. It looks so
completely medieval that film crews use it as a backdrop
to historical romances or adventures. Yet the castle is
both more and less historical than it looks. The great
Whin Sill crag has been defended since the Iron Age; this
became the site of a fort for the invading Anglians in
AD 547 and was given by King Ethelfrith to his wife
Bebba – Bebba's burgh became Bamburgh.

An eventful progress through the centuries ensued:

COAL FROM THE SEA
The coal seams near Amble
run out under the North Sea,
often very close to the surface
of the seabed. After winter
storms coal can sometimes be
found littering the shoreline,
providing free fuel for local
people. The open-cast
coalmines that formerly
occupied large areas of land in
the Amble area have now
been reclaimed.

*Bamburgh Castle is a
dramatic landmark, visible
for miles along the
Northumberland coast*

THE HOLY BEAM

St Aidan of Lindisfarne died at Bamburgh on 31 August AD 651, in a tent next to the church. 'As he drew his last breath,' says Bede, 'He was leaning against a post that buttressed the wall'. This post subsequently survived two fires, and was put inside the rebuilt church as a relic. 'Many have cut chips of wood and put them in water, by which many have been cured of their diseases.' The same forked beam is said still to be in the tower ceiling of St Aidan's Church.

Northumbrian kings were crowned here, the fortress was sacked by the Vikings, then fell easily to the Normans, who began the stone castle we now see. The great keep was built in the 1150s, and additions were made in later centuries, creating a castle which was virtually impregnable until in 1464, when it became the first castle ever to be taken by artillery. It was Edward IV's army who shelled it into submission.

The shattered remains passed to the local Forster family during the time of James I & VI, and they held it – but largely left it derelict – until the early 18th century, when Lord Crewe, Bishop of Durham, took charge. He undertook some repairs and left the castle as a charitable trust, run by Dr John Sharpe. The good doctor restored the ruins and ran an early welfare state in Bamburgh, with a free school, an infirmary, a free lending library and a windmill that sold cheap flour – its tower can still be seen in the grounds.

The castle was sold in 1894 to Lord Armstrong, Victorian inventor and industrialist (see Cragside, page 52). It is his restorations that make the castle seem so complete today – and perhaps a little disappointing to today's visitors. The State Rooms seem late Victorian, and though they are undeniably palatial, particularly the Great Hall with its impressive hammer-beam roof and musicians' gallery, they do not live up to the promise of the exterior. However, there is a fine display of armour from the Tower of London, portraits, furniture and porcelain – as well as the chains used by Dr Sharpe's early coastguard and lifeboat service.

Bamburgh village can be extremely busy at the height of the tourist season, but is a pleasant place for a stroll. The parish church stands on the site of a chapel used by St Aidan and has a beautiful early 13th-century chancel and Forster family monuments, as well as Grace Darling's much-visited grave in the churchyard. Bamburgh also has an attractive sandy beach and a spectacularly sited golf course at Budle Point, with views to Holy Island. Budle Bay, an area of wetland west of Bamburgh, is a nature reserve visited by many wildfowl – information boards will help to identify them.

An effigy of Grace Darling adorns the heroine's tomb in Bamburgh churchyard

BERWICK-UPON-TWEED Northumberland Map ref
NT9953
Berwick-upon-Tweed was a Royal Burgh of Scotland until
William the Lion surrendered it to the English in 1174.
Over the next 300 years it changed hands eleven times,
became a free town in 1482 and an independent state
within England in 1502. Until 1746 Acts of Parliament
did not apply to Berwick unless they said so. It only
became legally part of Northumberland in 1974.

*The sturdy Elizabethan
ramparts are unique to
Berwick, but were never put
to the test*

Such a turbulent past gives Berwick its own gritty individuality. A fascinating town, of unexpected levels and grey stone houses, it holds a unique place in both British and military history. In the Middle Ages it was protected at its north end by the castle, first mentioned in 1160 and rebuilt at the end of the 13th century. Its White Wall plunges from the castle to the river, protecting precipitous steps known as 'The Breakynecks'. The Constable's Tower remains impressive, and you can see part of the northwest wall perfectly from the station platform – much more was demolished when the railway reached Berwick. A plaque records Edward I's decision in the Great Hall in 1292 to give the crown of Scotland to John Baliol and not to Robert the Bruce.

Berwick had medieval town walls – the best remaining stretch is along the cliffs between Meg's Mount and the railway bridge – but more important are the Elizabethan ramparts. Built between 1558 and 1569, when the Scots and the French were threatening England, they are unique in Britain. The walk along them should not be missed, to see the 22-foot (6.7m) high stone-faced walls, 12 feet (3.6m) thick at the base and topped with grassed mounds. Their huge arrow-head bastions enabled cannon to shoot straight out and along the flanking walls. They were never properly finished. In 1568 Mary, Queen of Scots, fled to England, removing some of the Scottish threat – and when James I & VI became king in 1603 they were redundant.

Berwick remained a military town, however, and Britain's earliest barracks, dating from the early 17th century, were built to house nearly 600 men. Apparently, the locals objected to soldiers being billeted in public houses. The barracks were designed by Vanbrugh,

A walk around the town's medieval ramparts is a 'must' for any visitor

architect of Blenheim Palace and Castle Howard, and now contain two museums – the King's Own Scottish Borderers Museum and the town Museum and Art Gallery, which, alongside exhibits of local history, has something of a surprise – there are outstanding works of art here, including Chinese ceramics, medieval carvings and paintings by Degas and Daubigny, presented by Sir William Burrell, founder of the more famous Glasgow Burrell Collection. Modern art is displayed at the Gymnasium Gallery on the Parade.

Opposite the Barracks is Berwick parish church – rare for being built in the 1650s, during the Commonwealth. Oliver Cromwell, a friend of the church's benefactor, hated bells, so there is no tower. Bells did arrive in Berwick, but were hung in the mid-18th century Guildhall, Berwick's most prominent building, with its columned front and tall tower and spire.

Among Berwick's many landmarks are its bridges. A wooden bridge was swept away in 1199, and two more in the next century. Without one for 200 years, Berwick put up another wooden bridge in Tudor times, but it was James I & VI, going to London in 1603, who demanded, and eventually paid for, the magnificent 1,164-foot (355.4m) long Old Bridge. It remained the only road bridge until the Royal Tweed Bridge was built in 1928, but the most spectacular of Berwick's bridges, Robert Stephenson's Royal Border Bridge, 2,152 feet (656m) long on 28 high arches, was built for the railway in 1846.

Tweedmouth's neighbour, Spittal, has a good beach, and Berwick harbour is busy with both leisure and commercial boats.

Berwick's mellow old bridges form a vital link with the rest of England

FISHING ON THE TWEED
The Tweed provides fine fishing for both salmon (expensive) and trout. It is classed as a Scottish water, so rod licences are not needed, although you must have a permit. Buy them, and ask for information, at a good local tackle shop – Game Fair in Marygate, Berwick, is recommended.

OLD TRADITIONS
Old traditions, including the Riding of the Bounds, starting from the Guildhall on 1 May each year, are preserved in Berwick, while just across the river in Tweedmouth the annual Festival in July includes the crowning of the Salmon Queen and a procession that passes through Berwick centre.

Northumberland's Coast and Hills

Castles, spectacular views of the Cheviots, wild moorland and the islands off the beautiful Northumberland coast are among the highlights of this circular drive from England's most northerly town. This is a tour of 75 miles (120.7km) – 10 miles (16-km) more if you visit Holy Island, but check on the tides before crossing the causeway.

ROUTE DIRECTIONS

See Key to Car Tours on page 120.

From the centre of Berwick-upon-Tweed go over the Royal Tweed Bridge, signed 'Newcastle, A1' and turn right, signed 'Coldstream A698'. Go right at the first roundabout and straight on at the second, following Coldstream signs. After 3 miles (4.8km), turn right along an unclassified road signed 'Norham Castle'.

In 2 miles (3.2km) pass the fine ruins of 12th-century **Norham Castle** and enter Norham. Follow the road past the cross and at the T-junction turn left on the B6470. After half a mile (800m) turn right along an unclassified road, signed 'Norham Station, Cornhill'. At the T-junction turn left on the A698, signed 'Berwick', then immediately right on to an unclassified road. Follow this winding road for 4 miles (6.4km), following signs for Etal and Ford, to reach the

B6354, where you turn right, signed 'Etal, Wooler'.

Follow the road for 3 miles (4.8km) through Etal, with its castle, to Ford – don't miss the murals at **Lady Waterford Hall** – ignoring the road right to Wooler. Just before Ford church turn right, signed 'Kimmerston'. After 1½ miles (2.4km) turn right at the T-junction, signed 'Milfield'. Go over Milfield Bridge and straight on to meet the A697, where you turn left towards Wooler and Morpeth.

Follow the main road beside the Cheviots through Akeld and at a junction turn right (signed 'Wooler light traffic only') then continue into the centre of Wooler, known as the 'Gateway to the Cheviots'. At the end of the main street turn left by the church then cross the main road on to the B6348, signed 'Chatton', 'Belford' and **'Chillingham Castle, Wild Cattle'**. After 2½ miles (4km)

St Cuthbert's cave, near Doddington, is known locally as Cuddy's Crag or Cove

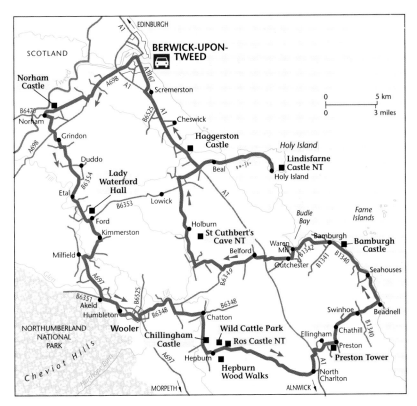

there is a sharp right-hand bend at the top of a hill. Beyond this, follow the main road, for 2½ miles (4km) to Chatton. Turn right at the 'Chillingham, Alnwick' sign. Follow the road past the entrance to the Wild Cattle Park and the 800-year-old castle and at the brow of the hill turn left, signed 'Hepburn Wood Walks'.

Follow the road through Hepburn over the cattle grid and uphill, past **Ros Castle**. The road needs care as it winds over the moorland for 7 miles (11.5km), because it is narrow, but wide verges allow for passing. The road descends into North Charlton. At the A1 turn left and after a mile (1.6km), turn right, signed 'Preston Tower, Ellingham'. After 2 miles

(3.2km) you will see **Preston Tower**, with its display of medieval border life. At the T-junction just beyond, turn left, signed 'Beadnell, Seahouses'.

Go over the level crossing, continue for 3½ miles (5.6km) past Bednell and along the coast on the B1340 (excellent views of the Farne Islands), into Seahouses. At the roundabout turn right, go along the main street then turn left, following the Coastal Route to Bamburgh. Pass Bamburgh Castle and the parish church. Go round Budle Bay and at the T-junction in Waren Mill turn left, signed 'Belford, Wooler'. In 2½ miles (4km) turn right on the A1 and then left into Belford.

Just before the church turn left on B6349 signed 'Wooler'. After 2½ miles (4km), turn

right along a narrow unclassified road signed 'Hazelrigg, Lowick'. There are spectacular views of the Cheviots from this road. Turn right at a T-junction after 2 miles (3.6km), signed 'Holburn, Berwick'. A little way along the road is the track to **St Cuthbert's Cave**. After 5 miles (8km) cross the B6353, then after half a mile (800m) turn right, signed 'Kentstone, Beal'.

At the A1 go straight over if you wish to visit **Holy Island** (check the tides); otherwise, turn left towards Berwick, passing Haggerston Castle. In 4½ miles (7.2km) turn right at the roundabout along the A1167, signed 'Berwick'. At the next roundabout go straight on, over the Royal Berwick Bridge and into the centre of the town.

PRIMEVAL CATTLE
The park at Chillingham, walled since 1220, contains wild cattle, descendants of a herd older than the castle itself. Like cattle that once roamed the primeval forests of Europe, they have white coats and black muzzles, with black tips to their horns. The dominant bull is the only one to sire calves, and fights with younger males until he is defeated, when he is banished alone to a distant part of the park. It was a former king bull that Thomas Bewick (see page 82) drew for his *History of Quadrupeds*, but in order to get a good look '... I was under the necessity of creeping on my hands and knees to leeward, and out of his sight' (he had earlier been chased up a tree by the dominant bull). The herd is now managed by a trust and the park is open to the public, though a good view of the cattle cannot be guaranteed – binoculars will help.

Looking at Chillingham Castle today it is easy to forget that it was a neglected shell until the 1980s

CHILLINGHAM   Northumberland Map ref NU0525

Chillingham village, with its Tudor-style houses, was built by the Earls of Tankerville, related by marriage to the Grey family. In the church is the tomb of 15th-century Sir Ralph Grey, with rare figures of saints that escaped the religious destruction of following centuries. The Greys fought against both the Scots and, often, the Percys of Alnwick. Their stronghold, Chillingham Castle, was started in 1245, and Henry III and Edward III were entertained here. Sir Thomas Grey gave it much of its present appearance in 1344, when it had a moat – now a huge tunnel under the south lawn.

Captured by Scots just before the Battle of Flodden in 1513, the castle was soon back in the Greys' hands. When they refused to join the Pilgrimage of Grace in 1536 (a northern rebellion against Henry VIII's Dissolution of the Monasteries) the Percys reduced it to a shell, but it was quickly repaired, and in the next century was extensively reconstructed; the cloister range in the courtyard, with statues of the Worthies, was added at that time.

Additions of 1753 and alterations after a fire in 1803 added to the castle's richness, but all was nearly lost when it was left empty after the contents were sold in 1933. There was another fire, in the north wing, during the time that soldiers were billeted here in the 1940s and rot ravaged the rest, until the 1980s, when Sir Humphrey Wakefield, related to the Greys, bought the castle and began its triumphant restoration.

Visitors can see the splendid Great Hall, with banners and armour, as well as antique furniture, tapestries and carefully restored plaster and metalwork, carving and masonry. There is even a torture chamber, suitable for 'the most haunted castle in England'. The gardens, too, have been restored after 50 years of neglect, and include woodland walks and a topiary garden on the site of the tournament ground.

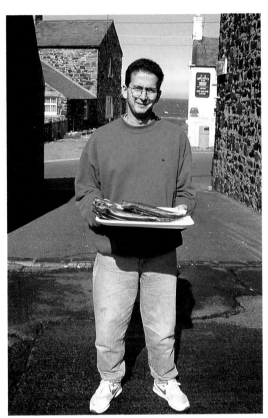

Craster oak-smoked kippers are famous, but the fresh fish is bought in from elsewhere along the coast

KIPPERS FROM CRASTER
Craster kippers have graced the best breakfast tables for more than 150 years. At Robson's, set above the harbour, four generations have cured herrings in smokehouses more than 130 years old. Although now more mechanised than when 'herring lassies' split and cleaned the fish, the process is the same. Fish are cleaned, salted and hung on tenter-sticks and placed high in the lumb (chimney) of the smokehouse, to cure for up to 16 hours above fires of whitewood shavings covered with oak sawdust. You can buy them on the premises and sample them – crabs, lobsters and smoked salmon, too – in the restaurant.

CRASTER Northumberland Map Ref NU2519
A picturesque village that seems to tumble into the sea, Craster was a fishing haven in the 17th century, although its harbour, today used by pleasure craft and traditional cobles, was given its present form in the 1900s. It was built by the local landowners – the Crasters – in memory of Captain Craster, killed on an expedition to Tibet in 1904. The trade it was involved in then was the export of whinstone (used for roads and kerbs), and you can still see the concrete arch that supported the chipping silos. The quarry is now the National Trust car park, a good starting point for walks to Dunstanburgh Castle (see page 26).

Howick Gardens, a mile (1.6km) south of Craster, surround a late-18th century house (not open), which was the home of the 2nd Earl Grey. As Prime Minister, he steered through the 1832 Parliamentary Reform Bill – and gave his name to Earl Grey tea. There is fine woodland with a network of paths and glades where rare plants and shrubs thrive – don't miss the rhododendron season – as well as lawns, a formal terrace with urns, and alpine beds.

Hill and Coast Views from an Iron-Age Fort

A handful of castles, coastal views from Berwick to Warkworth, the Cheviots and the Scottish Lowlands are your spectacular reward for this short walk. It is all on paths and tracks (may be muddy after rain), and two steep descents can be avoided by returning from Ros Castle viewpoint by the outward route.

Time: 1¼ hours. Distance: 2½ miles (4km).
Location: 10 miles (16km) northwest of Alnwick.
Start: Hepburn, southeast of Chillingham. Park in Forest Enterprise car park. (OS grid ref: NU072248.)
OS Map: Explorer 340
(Holy Island & Bamburgh, Wooler, Belford)
1:25,000.
See Key to Walks on page 121.

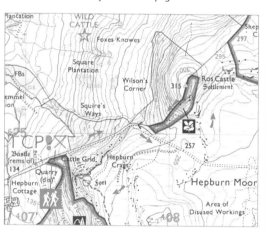

ROUTE DIRECTIONS

From the car park walk by the information sign, through a row of posts and on to the metalled lane. Pass over the cattle grid and continue up the hill, alongside a plantation, to its summit. Walk past a National Trust sign on the left to soon reach a marker post with an orange arrow. Turn left up the marked track, which curves right as it ascends the hill. Follow the track to approach the summit of the hill from the other side. The viewing platform at **Ros Castle**, with wide views in every direction, has topographs showing the main points of interest, including **Chillingham Castle and Park**.

From the Triangulation Pillar continue along the path, with the wall to the right, and follow the wall steeply downhill, taking great care on the rocky descent. (Alternatively, return by the path you came up). At the bottom of the steep slope make for the National Trust sign on the road and turn left. (To avoid the next steep descent, turn right to return to the car park down the lane). At the marker post where the hill ascent began, turn right and follow the track to the hill fort on **Hepburn Crags**. From the edge of the crags is a view of the **Bastle House**. Carefully descend the crags into woodland, go over a stile and down to a track. Turn right for the car park.

POINTS OF INTEREST

Ros Castle
Ros Castle is perhaps the most spectacular viewpoint in Northumbria, with a 360-degree view that, in good weather, allows you to see the whole sweep of the Northumberland coast, the Cheviot Hills and into Scotland. The topograph indicates the main points of interest, which include Holy Island, the Farne Islands, Bamburgh Castle, Dunstanburgh Castle, Warkworth Castle and Chillingham Castle and Park. Ros Castle itself is an Iron-Age hill fort with a single bank and double ditches. A beacon was set up here in the Napoleonic Wars, and when it was fired by accident in 1804 set off a widespread scare that the French were invading. Ros Castle was given to the National Trust in 1936 as part of a memorial to Sir Edward Grey, Foreign Secretary for ten years at the beginning of this century. On 3 August 1914, as war was about to be declared, he made the famous remark

Bastle House

Although known as Hepburn Bastle House, this fine ruin is unlike other bastles (derived from the French bastille) – it is actually a fortified tower of rather more aristocratic origins. It was built in the 15th century – the cross windows probably date from that time – and was later reconstructed with bigger windows in the slightly more peaceful times of the 16th century. The Bastle House can be seen particularly well from Hepburn Crags.

'The lamps are going out all over Europe; we shall not see them lit again in our lifetime'. In his retirement he often came to Ros Castle.

Chillingham's wild cattle are fierce and shy, in contrast to the peaceful Old English breed, also kept in the park

This pleasant walk from Hepburn ascends the two hills of Hepburn Crags and Ros Castle

Chillingham Castle and Park

One of the great Northumbrian castles, Chillingham, seen well from Ros Castle, was held by the Greys from 1245 and captured by the Scots before Flodden in 1513. Added to in the 17th and 18th centuries, it was left empty when its contents were sold in 1933. Now restored by a Grey descendant, it has fine interiors and a lovely garden. The Park, walled since 1220, holds the famous Chillingham White Cattle. Descendants of primeval beasts, they are mostly shy but can be fierce if angered.

Hepburn Crags

There are more fine views from the hill fort on Hepburn Crags, where a single bank on the plateau overlooks the River Till. The Crags are part of the Great Whin Sill, which further east forms the Farne Islands.

Three corner towers of the high keep of Dunstanburgh Castle still watch over the shore

FLODDEN FIELD...
The famous Scots lament, *The Flowers of the Forest*, commemorates 'Black Friday' – 9 September 1513 – when at least 9,000 of James IV's army were killed. He invaded England in the early summer, partly to help his French allies, who were fighting Henry VIII. After destroying Norham, Wark and Etal Castles he established his headquarters at Ford Castle. But the 18-day delay in getting from the borders to Ford gave the English, under the Earl of Surrey, time to muster, and for the Scots army to diminish to perhaps 30,000.

DUNSTANBURGH CASTLE Northumberland Map ref NU2622
The ruins of Dunstanburgh Castle are among the most romantically sited in Britain. In the Middle Ages sea surrounded the steep cliffs to the castle's north and filled the moat which had been dug around its more vulnerable sides. In area it is the largest castle in Northumbria – 11 acres – and was begun in 1314 by Thomas, Earl of Lancaster to protect a small harbour. His great gatehouse, largest of the surviving fragments, was turned into a keep by John of Gaunt in the 1380s. He built a new entrance to the west, making the castle less easy to attack. Taken and recaptured several times in its history, it fell into ruin in the 16th century. Dunstanburgh is said to be haunted by Sir Guy the Seeker, who failed to waken an enchanted princess here.

EDLINGHAM Northumberland Map ref NU1109
Set in a pleasant valley below Corby's Crags, Edlingham has one of Northumberland's many tower houses, though with a more complicated history than most. It was started by Sir William Felton at the very end of the 13th century, then about 50 years later came the surviving tower with its impressive fireplaces, as well as a gatehouse, later altered. Sir William is buried in the church – typically Northumbrian, with a strong, low tower and a nave from around 1060.
  In Thrunton Wood, 2½ miles (4km) west, are forest walks and picnic sites. Callay Crag has an artificial cave, the hiding place of a 17th-century priest, and on Castle Hill are Iron-Age earthworks and the remains of a pele.

ETAL AND FORD Northumberland Map ref
NT9339/NT9437

Etal and its neighbour Ford have all the ingredients for a good family day out. Etal has Northumberland's only thatched pub, the Black Bull, and the Post Office serves teas with home baking. The village's main street is a pretty mix of thatched and stone-tiled cottages, and leads to Etal Castle, the ruins of a border tower-house of the early 14th century. Scottish guns were dragged back to damaged Etal after the Battle of Flodden, and an exhibition in a former chapel in the grounds has displays about that battle and the Border Wars in general.

In nearby Heatherslaw the water-powered corn mill is an 18th- and 19th-century building on a site used for at least 700 years. Milling is demonstrated, and stone-ground flour and locally baked products are on sale. Heatherslaw also boasts a 15-inch gauge steam railway that runs for almost 2 miles (3.2km) alongside the River Till.

Ford owes much of its model village atmosphere to Louisa, Countess of Waterford, who lived at Ford Castle and spent most of her widowhood caring for the villagers. The 14th-century castle (not open) was added to in the 18th century – the Portcullis Gate dates from 1791 – and in the 1860s by Lady Waterford. She was a famous beauty (she met her husband at the Eglinton Tournament in Ayrshire in 1839) and a friend of artists. The Lady Waterford Hall has murals of Biblical scenes she painted in watercolour on paper, using locals as her models – the joiner's son as Jesus and her gamekeeper as St Paul. She was also responsible for the blacksmith's forge, with its horseshoe doorway. Her memorial is in the churchyard.

Etal and Ford and their surrounding villages have a wide variety of craft, food and plant shops, and opportunities for fishing and riding.

...THE BATTLE
The Scots gathered for battle on Flodden Hill, 4 miles (6.4km) west of Ford, but the Earl of Surrey sent part of his force to cut off the Scots' retreat northwards. James IV might have won if he had launched his attack during this manoeuvre, but he delayed fatally and faced the attack from the north, near Branxton. Fighting began at 4pm and by nightfall the Scots had been defeated, despite brave fighting. Among the dead were James and his son, twelve earls, 15 clan chiefs, a bishop and two abbots – as well as 5,000 English. The site of the battle is marked with a modern cross, inscribed 'FLODDEN 1513. TO THE BRAVE OF BOTH NATIONS'.

Lady Waterford's paintings of Biblical subjects which line the old school hall at Ford show the influence of the Pre-Raphaelite artists

SHOTGUN WEDDINGS

Weddings are rare on Holy Island, but those that do occur retain unusual traditions. After the service the bride is taken to the east end of the church. There the two oldest men on the island help her to jump over a luck-giving stone called the petting stool – the higher the jump the better the bride's fortune and fertility. Shotguns are fired to scare away evil influences, and the married couple are only released from the churchyard on payment of a fine. At the reception there is often Lindisfarne mead, once the drink of the monks and now made commercially on the island, and the bride has to endure another ordeal. A plate of wedding cake is thrown over her head – if the plate breaks, her happiness is assured.

ISLAND WILDLIFE

Holy Island forms part of the Lindisfarne Nature Reserve, which has sand dunes and mudflats that are home to a wide variety of birds. It is the only place in Great Britain where the light-bellied type of Brent geese overwinter, and there are many other species to be seen on or near the island, including oyster-catchers, wigeon, ducks, curlews, godwits, dunlins, turnstones and knots. Among the wild flowers that may be seen are several species of wild orchid and hellebore. Always stick to the paths provided and do not pick wild flowers or disturb the birds or other wildlife.

HOLY ISLAND Northumberland Map ref NU1241

Holy Island has been known as such since the 11th century, although its Celtic name, Lindisfarne, is just as familiar. Holy it certainly was, because this was one of the main centres of Christianity in the Dark Ages. The island was given to St Aidan in AD 635 by Oswald, King of Northumbria, and it became well respected throughout Europe.

Even more famous and influential was St Cuthbert, whose life and teaching were a magnet for pilgrims. He died in AD 687 and was buried in the church, but when it was sacked during Danish raids in AD 875 the monks fled with his bones, wandering through Northumbria in search of a safe and permanent home for them. St Cuthbert's remains eventually arrived in Durham more than 100 years later (see page 85), but his memory is still kept alive in Holy Island – fossilised crinoids washed ashore are locally called St Cuthbert's beads, and eider ducks are his chicks.

Lindisfarne seems ideal for the monastic life – bare, windswept and flat, surrounded by sands which are covered by tides twice a day. Before crossing to the island via the causeway, check the tide tables – here, in Tourist Information Offices or in the local newspapers – and take note of the warning signs. A refuge is provided for the foolhardy who don't. The old pilgrims' route from the mainland is marked by posts leading almost directly to the village, a mixture of traditional houses and modern bungalows.

South of the square is St Mary's Church. On show there is a copy of the famous *Lindisfarne Gospels* (the original is in the British Museum), illuminated here in about AD 698 and kept for centuries in Durham. Just off shore is St Cuthbert's Island, used by the saint when he felt the need for more solitude than was available on the main island. It can be reached at low tide, and a simple cross marks his chapel.

Next to the church are the remains of Lindisfarne Priory, built of beautiful red sandstone, weathered into gullies and ripples. Founded by the Bishop of Durham in 1083, and finished by 1140, it has columns like Durham Cathedral, patterned with zigzags and chequers. The remaining rib of the crossing, known as the rainbow arch, shows that it once had a strong tower. Part of the cloister remains – in contrasting grey stone – but there is not much more, except a gatehouse and defensive walls against the Scots. The nearby museum tells the story of the island and its place in the religious life of the country. Stones from the Priory were used in the 1540s to build a fort on Beblowe, a rocky crag on the south shore. Its purpose was to defend the harbour, where part of Henry VIII's fleet had sheltered in 1543 and where today the boats of lobster and crab fishermen mingle with pleasure craft. These defences were never tested before peace with the Scots came 60 years later. Apart

from its capture for one night in 1715 by two opportunist Jacobites, it was neglected until Edward Hudson, founder of *Country Life* magazine, bought it in 1902 and commissioned the architect Edwin Lutyens to adapt it for use as a home.

Now owned by the National Trust, it shows Lutyens at his most inventive, hollowing rooms out of unexpected corners, some like the inside of an upturned stone boat. The Upper Battery gives fine views of the island, the Farne Islands and the mainland. Lutyens' gardening collaborator Gertrude Jekyll designed the tiny walled garden 500 yards (457m) north of the castle. Above the beach to the southeast of the castle are Victorian lime kilns.

Edwin Lutyens' romantic restoration of Lindisfarne Castle evoked a comfortable 17th-century style

The versatile Small Pipes of Northumbria have enjoyed a revival of interest in recent years

BAGS OF WIND

Bagpipes are not the sole preserve of Scotland, as Morpeth Chantry Bagpipe Museum proves. It has 120 sets, of all shapes and sizes and from all around the world, and visitors can hear their sounds and characteristic music on special headphones. Northumbrian Small Pipes have a special place here. Blown not by the mouth but by bellows under the arm, they are sweeter-voiced and less raucous than their northern cousins. They can be heard at events like Morpeth Northumberland Gathering, a festival of traditional music, song and dance held each April.

MORPETH Northumberland Map ref NZ1986

Morpeth's town centre has attractive alleys and courtyards, and some fine old buildings, including the Town Hall by Vanbrugh, rebuilt after a fire in the 19th century, and the Clock Tower in the middle of Oldgate, erected in the early 17th century. Before the days of bypasses, the 19th-century bridge used to take A1 traffic over the River Wansbeck into the town. In the bridge chapel, the Chantry, with its tearoom and Tourist Information Centre, more than 40 craftsmen display their work. The Northumberland Wildlife Trust runs a shop and there are two museums.

St Mary's Church has the best stained glass in Northumberland, dating, like the church, from the 14th century. Its churchyard, with a watch house to prevent body snatching, contains the grave of Suffragette Emily Davison, who died when she threw herself under the hooves of George V's horse at the 1913 Derby meeting. St James's Church, three quarters of mile (1.2km) north, is an impressive Victorian neo-Norman building.

Morpeth has had two castles. The earlier, on Ha' Hill near St Mary's, was not rebuilt after King John burned the town in 1261. Of the second, on Castle Walk, sections of the wall and a large gatehouse, mostly 15th-century, survive. Near by in colourful Carlisle Park is the Courthouse, once the gateway to the gaol.

Mitford, west of Morpeth, has a fine church in woodland and the remains of a mainly 12th-century castle. Nearer Morpeth is Newminster Abbey, one of the richest Cistercian abbeys in the north, with vast sheep runs on the Cheviots. Little remains today except part of the Chapter House, beautifully set among grass, wild flowers and brambles.

NORHAM Northumberland Map ref NT9047

Turner often painted the ruins of Norham Castle, which guards an important ford across the Tweed into Scotland. Built about 1158, Norham was the Bishop of Durham's chief northern stronghold – the area was known as Norhamshire and was part of County Durham, not Northumberland. The great red sandstone keep was battered into surrender by the Scottish army before Flodden, and the Marmion Gate is a reminder that Sir Walter Scott set his poem about the battle here. An earlier Scottish king, William the Lion, agreed to pay tribute money to King John here in 1209, and the castle was besieged unsuccessfully for 40 days by Alexander II five years later. Edward I declared himself Paramount King of Scotland at Norham, where Robert the Bruce and John Baliol were chosen finalists in the King of Scotland competition. The final was at Berwick-upon-Tweed.

In the village St Cuthbert's Church shows the rich influence of the Durham Bishops, with a chancel of about 1170, Norman nave arches like part of Durham Castle and the 17th-century vicar's stall and the pulpit which were formerly in Durham Cathedral. The cross on the village green has a medieval base and 19th-century top. Norham Station has a working signal box, a good model railway and a collection of Victoriana.

KEEPING UP THE SUSPENSE

Union Bridge, 2 miles (3.2km) northeast of Norham, was Europe's first suspension bridge to carry vehicles. Still in use and now a scheduled Ancient Monument, it was designed by Captain Brown, who had patented its chain links in 1817, and opened in 1820. Its span is 480 feet (146m) and the wooden road hangs from link bars only two inches (five centimetres) thick. The chains are attached to a tall arch on the Scottish side of the Tweed, but to a rock in England. Constructed in just eleven months, the bridge cost £7,000 – a third of the cost of a stone bridge.

*'Day set on Norham's castled steep
And Tweed's fair river, broad and deep...'*
– *Scott,* **Marmion** *(1808)*

PRESTON TOWER   Northumberland Map ref NU1827
Robert Harbottle's pele tower of the 1390s suffered the
ignominy of having two of its four towers demolished in
1603, 90 years after Sir Guiscard Harbottle died at
Flodden in hand-to-hand fighting with the Scots King
James IV. It was rescued from decay and encroaching
farm buildings in 1864, but only so that it could hold
water tanks for the Georgian house near by.

The tower has a more dignified existence today,
housing displays about the Battle of Flodden and its
impact, as well as recreating the uncomfortable and
spartan life of the Border Reivers at the beginning of the
15th century.

GREY SEALS

The Farne Islands are one of
only two places on Britain's
east coast where grey seals
breed, and there have been
seals here since at least the
12th century. These
inquisitive animals are
frequently seen observing
their many visitors from the
safety of the rocks or with
their heads bobbing among
the waves. Grey seals can
grow up to 9½ feet (3m) long
and weigh as much as 600lb
(273kg). They produce their
pups, with their white, long-
haired coats, between
September and December.
The mothers look after them
on land and teach them to
swim, then the colonies
disperse – pups born at the
Farne Islands are often found
as adults in Norway.

SEAHOUSES AND THE FARNE ISLANDS
Northumberland Map ref NU2231/NU2338

In 1858 Seahouses was referred to as 'a common-looking
town, squalid in places', but today it has a much more
prosperous quality, geared to the tourist industry. In the
town there are some pleasant fishermen's cottages
around Craster Square and a busy harbour, which was
originally built in the 18th century, but was much
enlarged in the 19th. Seahouses harbour is the place to
get boat trips to the Farne Islands, and there are fine
sands both to the north and the south of the sheltering
Snook Point. A mile (1.6km) south of Seahouses is
Beadnell, which has an 18th-century church and a pub –
the Craster Arms – with a large carved coat of arms

*Lobster boats at rest in the
sheltered harbour at
Seahouses*

on its front wall and the remains of a medieval tower at the back. Above the harbour – the only one on the east coast that faces west – is the site of the medieval St Ebba's chapel and an impressive group of lime-kilns which date from 1798.

St Aidan spent each Lent on Inner Farne, one of the 28 Farne Islands (or 15, if you count at high tide), and St Cuthbert lived here from AD 676 to AD 685. His cell on Inner Farne was surrounded by an embankment so that all he could see was heaven. It was his expressed wish to be buried here, but his body was taken instead to Lindisfarne. The present St Cuthbert's Church on Inner Farne, near the site of his hermitage, dates mostly from about 1370 and has 17th-century woodwork which was brought here from Durham Cathedral in the 19th century. To the west is Prior Castell's Tower, which may have held a lighthouse from the days when there were Benedictine monks on the island. Today's white-painted lighthouse was built in 1809.

Further out, beyond Staple, is Longstone, an uninviting, low, bare rock with a red and white striped lighthouse, built in 1826. This was where the Darling family lived, and from where Grace and her father set out on their famous rescue mission.

For many visitors the attraction of the Farne Islands is their wildlife, especially the birds and the seals. Egg collectors were causing great damage in the 19th century, and the Farne Islands Association, set up in 1880, employed watchers to protect the breeding birds. The National Trust has owned the islands since 1925, and permits to land on Inner Farne and Staple Island (the only ones where it is allowed), must be bought from

GRACE DARLING

Grace Darling's father was keeper of the Longstone lighthouse. Before dawn on 7 September 1838 the consumptive Grace rowed with her father to the 400-ton luxury passenger-steamer *Forfarshire*, which had gone aground on Big Harcar in a northerly gale. Before the Seahouses lifeboat, with Grace's brother aboard, arrived, they had saved nine lives, and Grace became a national heroine, her fame assured by her early death four years later at the age of 27. Wordsworth wrote that she was 'Pious and pure, modest and yet so brave'. The boat used for the daring rescue, a locally built coble, 21 feet (6.4m) long, is now in the Grace Darling Museum in Bamburgh.

Grey seal pups in pale, silvery fur defy their name

Seals flop on the rocks by the Longstone lighthouse, a spot famously associated with Grace Darling

the Wardens. Check, too, that your boatman is licensed to land his passengers. During the breeding season, from May to July, landing is restricted – and if the weather is bad you may not be able to land at all. There are nature walks on both these islands.

The great dolerite rocks that form the Farne Islands are the easternmost part of the Great Whin Sill, and are home to at least 17 species of bird, which perch precariously on the cliffs or wheel noisily overhead – you should always wear a hat when visiting these islands! The delightful little puffins are always favourites, but you may also see fulmars, petrels, razorbills, ring plover, rock pipits, eiders (known hereabouts as St Cuthbert's – or Cuddy's – Chicks), kittiwakes, terns, guillemots, shags, cormorants, oystercatchers and, of course, gulls. The boat trips usually pass near enough to see their nesting sites, and on Staple and Inner Farne you can walk – with care – among their nests.

WARKWORTH Northumberland Map ref NU2406
Shakespeare, who set three scenes of his *Henry IV* here, called the ruins of magnificent Warkworth Castle 'this worm-eaten hold of ragged stone'. Actually, the huge keep is one of the most spectacular in Britain. Set in a loop of the River Coquet on the original motte, its plan is a cross superimposed on a square, and it stands to its

THE BEST APPROACH
Try, if you can, to approach Warkworth from the north, along the A1068 from Alnwick. It affords what Nikolaus Pevsner called 'one of the most exciting sequences of views one can have in England'. And if you take your trip in the spring, you will be well rewarded by the sight of hundreds of daffodils blooming on the steep-sided slopes of the castle mound.

full height, partly restored in the 19th century for use by the Duke of Northumberland. The original 11th-century structure on the motte was replaced by a stone castle before 1158 and was sacked by the Scots in 1174. The Great Gate Tower, guarding the vulnerable south approach, was built in around 1200, as was the Carrickfergus Tower to the west. The Percys lived at Warkworth rather than Alnwick until the 16th century – Hotspur was brought up here – and the Lion Tower, by the remains of the Great Hall in the outer ward, carries their crest.

The Percy Lion is also carved on the keep wall that dominates the little town, where the medieval street plan is still evident. Georgian and Victorian houses lead down the hill to the church and the fortified bridge. The Old Pretender was proclaimed here in 1715, his army dined at the Masons' Arms and his Catholic chaplain said prayers in the church.

The church has a 14th-century spire – spires are rare in Northumberland – but inside it is almost completely Norman, with a nave more than 90 feet (27.5m) long and an unusual stone-vaulted chancel, its roof ribs decorated with sharp-cut zigzags. This now peaceful church was the scene of a terrible massacre in 1174, when the Scottish army, under Earl Duncan, slaughtered most of the population of Warkworth, who had taken refuge within its walls.

HERMIT'S COMFORT

In summer take the short boat trip from the riverbank to Warkworth Hermitage, hewn from the rock face above the river in the 14th century. This was once called home by a hermit whose work was to pray for the Percy family. In the little Chapel the altar and all the columns are part of the rock, and the hermit also had a Sacristy with an additional altar. A hall, solar and kitchen are later additions – with such un-hermitical extras as fireplace, oven and lavatory. Mournful texts about gall and tears decorate the hermitage, which was occupied from about 1320 to the 1540s, when religious upheaval did away with hermits.

Warkworth's great keep, dating from 1390, is one of England's finest

Castle and Coast at Warkworth

'One of the most exciting sequences of views one can have in England', says Sir Nikolaus Pevsner about Warkworth. This walk takes you round the town and the castle, to the view of the Hermitage and to the coast, with its views of Coquet Island. Mostly easy walking along paths and seashore. A short roadside section needs care, especially with children.

Time: 2½ hours. Distance: 4 miles (6.4km).
Location: 5 miles (8km) southeast of Alnwick.
Start: In the centre of Warkworth, near the Market Cross.
Alternative parking near the beach. (OS grid ref: NU247061.)
OS Map: Explorer 332 Alnwick & Amble, Craster & Whittingham 1:25,000.
See Key to Walks on page 121.

ROUTE DIRECTIONS

From the Market Cross in **Warkworth**, walk down Bridge Street towards the River Coquet. At the river, go through the archway and over the old bridge. Cross the main road and go up the road opposite, signed 'Beach'. Follow the road for half a mile (800m) and as it bears left go straight ahead, down on to a track leading through the dunes on to the beach. To the right **Coquet Island** and **Amble** harbour can be seen.

Turn left and walk along the beach for three quarters of a mile (1.2km), then turn left on to the dunes and go up through the valley, under a footbridge and through a gate on to a track. Go straight forward. Just before the road, turn left down a path joining the road further down. Walk with care through Birling back to the river.

Cross the old bridge and go through the arch, turning right immediately afterwards, following a footpath signed 'Monks Walk'. Follow the path which leads past the parish church and where the path divides take the right fork, still along the river below the castle. Walk on for three quarters of a mile (1.2km), and go through a kissing gate. On the far bank of the river, opposite the seat, is Warkworth Hermitage.

At the footpath signpost turn left uphill to a kissing

Warkworth's lovely Old Bridge spans the River Coquet and once formed part of the town's fortifications

gate and bear left. Just before the road junction turn left along a footpath behind houses, signed 'Warkworth Castle'. Go behind the houses towards the castle, through a kissing gate and across two fields to another gate at the end of a wall. Through the gate go diagonally right to the entrance to the castle.

From the entrance continue down the metalled drive to the gate and turn left on to the road. As the road bends left around the castle go straight ahead in front of the Sun Hotel and take a footpath to the right of Roxbro House. Follow the passageway between the gardens, downhill towards the river, through a brick arch and turn left at a gap in the fence and go through a rose garden. At Bridge Street turn left to return to the market place and the start of the walk.

POINTS OF INTEREST

Warkworth

The castle, dominating the village, was the main home of the Percy family until the 16th century, and was mostly built in the 12th and 13th centuries. The 14th-century Old Bridge, with its defensive tower, is one of the country's very few fortified bridges. Only 11 feet (3.5m) wide, it carried all traffic into and out of Warkworth for almost 600 years until 1965. The medieval passageway, followed towards the end of the walk, shows how the layout of Warkworth remains as it was in the Middle Ages, with the houses on long garden strips. A few now have modern houses built on them, but the others are used today much as they were then, for growing vegetables and keeping hens and livestock.

The parish church, an almost complete Norman building, is where villagers were massacred in 1174, while in the rock-hewn Hermitage on the river bank below the castle a solitary monk prayed for the souls of the Percy family.

Coquet Island

Coquet Island was occupied by monks from at least the 7th century. The island had Northumberland's earliest-known windmill, in about 1200. The remains of medieval monastic buildings, home to monks from Tynemouth Priory, are now part of the lighthouse complex, built in 1841. Grace Darling's brother was once lighthouse keeper on Coquet Island. It is now an RSPB reserve, with large numbers of eider ducks, terns and puffins. Landing is not permitted here, but it is possible to take boat trips around the island to view the wildlife.

Amble

A former coal port, Amble's harbour is now busy with the pleasure boats which tie up in its marina. Boats leave here for trips round Coquet Island. The great sheltering breakwaters were built in the 1840s to designs by the engineer Rennie.

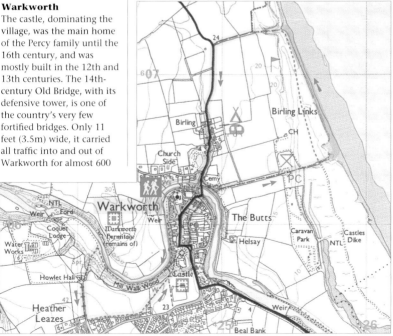

The Coast

Leisure Information

Places of Interest

Shopping

The Performing Arts

Sports, Activities and the Outdoors

Annual Events and Customs

Checklist

Leisure Information

TOURIST INFORMATION CENTRES

Adderstone
Adderstone Services, Belford.
Tel: 01668 213678.
Alnwick
The Shambles. Tel: 01665
510665.
Amble
Queen Street Car Park.
Tel: 01665 712313 (seasonal).
Berwick-upon-Tweed
106 Marygate. Tel: 01289
330733.
Craster
Car Park. Tel: 01665 576007
(seasonal).
Morpeth
The Chantry, Bridge Street.
Tel: 01670 511323.
Seahouses
Car Park, Seafield Road.
Tel: 01665 720884 (seasonal).

OTHER INFORMATION

**Regional Tourist
Information**
www.visitnorthumbria.com
English Heritage
Tel: 0870 333 1181
www.english-heritage.org.uk
**National Trust for
Northumbria**
Scots' Gap, Morpeth.
Northumberland.

Tel: 01670 774691.
www.nationaltrust.org.uk
**Northumberland Wildlife
Trust**
Garden House, St Nicholas Park,
Jubilee Road, Newcastle upon
Tyne. Tel: 0191 284 6884.
www.wildlifetrust.org.uk/
northumberland
Northumbria Water
Abbey Road, Pity Me, Durham.
Tel: 0191 383 2222.
www.nwl.co.uk

ORDNANCE SURVEY MAPS

Landranger 1:50,000 Sheets 74,
75, 81

Places of Interest

There will be an admission
charge at the following places
of interest unless otherwise
stated.
Alnwick Castle
Tel: 01665 510777. Open:
Castle Apr–Oct daily; park daily.
Park free.
Bamburgh Castle
Tel: 01668 214515. Open mid-
Mar to late Oct daily.
Berwick Barracks
Berwick-upon-Tweed. Tel:
01289 304493. Open Apr–Oct
daily; Nov–Mar most days.
Berwick Castle
Berwick-upon-Tweed. Open any

reasonable time. Free.
Chillingham Castle
Tel: 01668 215359. Open
May–Sep most days.
**Chillingham Wild Cattle
Park**
Tel: 01668 215250. Open
Apr–Oct most days.
Dunstanburgh Castle
Craster. Tel: 01665 576231.
Open Apr–Oct daily; Nov–Mar
certain days.
Edlingham Castle
Open any reasonable time.
Free.
Etal Castle
Etal Village. Tel: 01890 820332.
Open Apr–Oct daily.
Farne Islands
Inner Farne and Staple Island.
Tel: 01665 721099. Open Apr–
Sep daily. Boat trips to the
islands leave from Seahouses
harbour.Wear a hat.
Grace Darling Museum
Radcliffe Road, Bamburgh. Tel:
01668 214465. Open
Easter–Oct daily. Free.
**Guildhall and Cell Block
Museum**
Berwick-upon-Tweed. Tel:
01289 330900. Open
Easter–Sep, weekdays only.
Guided tours twice daily unless
closed for events.
Heatherslaw Corn Mill
Ford. Tel: 01890 820338. Open

Apr–Oct daily.
Heatherslaw Light Railway
Ford Forge, Heatherslaw,
Cornhill-upon-Tweed. Tel:
01890 820244. Open Apr–Oct
daily.
Howick Hall Gardens
Craster. Tel: 01665 577285.
Open Apr–Oct daily.
Lady Waterford Hall
Ford. Tel: 01890 820224. Open
Apr–Oct daily, Nov–Mar by
appointment.
Lindisfarne Castle
Holy Island. Tel: 01289 389244.
Open Apr–Oct according to
tides (telephone before visit).
Lindisfarne Priory
Holy Island. Tel: 01289 389200.
Open all year, daily.
**Morpeth Chantry Bagpipe
Museum**
Bridge Street. Tel: 01670
519466. Open all year, daily
except Sun.
Museum and Art Gallery
Ravensdowne Barracks, Berwick-
upon-Tweed. Tel: 01289
301869. Open Apr–Oct, daily;
Nov–Mar, Wed–Sun.
**Museum of the King's Own
Scottish Borderers**
The Barracks, Berwick-upon-
Tweed. Tel: 01289 307426.
Open all year, daily except Sun.
Norham Castle
Norham. Tel: 01661 881297.
Open Apr–Oct daily.
Norham Station Museum
Norham, near Berwick-upon-
Tweed. Tel: 01289 382217.
Open Easter and Jun–Sep certain
days.
Paxton House
Berwick-upon-Tweed. Tel:
01289 386291. Open Apr–Oct,
daily.
Preston Tower
Tel: 01665 589227. Open all
year, daily.
St Cuthbert's Cave
Belford. 3 miles (4.8 km) west.
Open any reasonable time. Free.
Warkworth Castle
Warkworth. Tel: 01665 711423.
Open all year, daily.
Warkworth Hermitage
Open Apr–Sep, certain days.
Wine & Spirit Museum
Palace Green, Berwick-upon-
Tweed. Tel: 01289 305153.
Open all year, most days. Free.

SPECIAL INTEREST FOR
CHILDREN

The following places may be of
interest to visitors with children.
Unless otherwise stated there
will be an admission charge.
Chain Bridge Honey Farm
Horncliffe, near Berwick-upon-
Tweed. Tel: 01289 386362.
Observation hives, vintage
tractors, displays about bees and
honey. Open daily, except
winter weekends. Free.
**Marine Life Centre and
Fishing Museum**
Main Street, Seahouses. Tel:
01665 721257. Seawater
aquarium, fishermen's museum
and cottage, touch tank where
children can handle small crabs.
Open Mar–Oct daily.

Shopping

Alnwick
Crafts and antiques. Open-air
market, Sat.
Amble
Quayside market, Sun.
Berwick-upon-Tweed
Open-air market, Wed and Sat.
Etal
Crafts, foods and plant shops.
Ford
Crafts, foods and plant shops.
Morpeth
Open-air market, Mon and Wed.

LOCAL SPECIALITIES
Crafts
Shire Pottery, Millers Yard,
Prudhoe Street, Alnwick. Pottery,
porcelain, art, furniture. Tel:
01665 602277.
Belford Craft Gallery, 2 Market

Place, Belford. Tel: 01668
213888. Pottery, furniture,
woodwork, paintings, books,
Northumbrian music, occasional
concerts.
Northumbria Craft Centre, The
Chantry, Morpeth. Tel: 01670
511217. Crafts including Celtic
knitwear and jewellery.
Fishing Tackle
Greys, Willowburn, Alnwick. Tel:
01665 510020. Fishing rod
manufacturers.
House of Hardy, Willowburn,
Alnwick. Tel: 01665 602771.
Museum of fishing tackle, shop,
factory tours by arrangement.
Food and Drink
Chain Bridge Honey Farm,
Horncliffe, near Berwick-upon-
Tweed. Tel: 01289 386362.
L Robson and Sons Ltd, Craster.
Kippers and smoked fish. Tel:
01665 576044.
Lindisfarne Limited, St Aidans
Winery, Holy Island. Mead,
honey and fudge. Tel: 01289
389230.
Ironwork and Woodwork
Errol Hut Smithy and Wood
Workshop, Letham Hill, Etal.
Tel: 01890 820317.

The Performing Arts

Alnwick
Playhouse, Bondgate Without,
Alnwick. Tel: 01665 510785.
Berwick-upon-Tweed
The Maltings Theatre and Arts,
Eastern Lane. Tel: 01289
330999.

*Colourful boats crowd the
jetties at Amble marina*

Sports, Activities and the Outdoors

ANGLING

Coarse and Fly
Information about fishing in the area is available from Tourist Information Centres and local tackle shops.

Sea
Alnmouth: Enquire at harbour.
Amble: Enquire at harbour.
Berwick-upon-Tweed: Shore fishing is restricted because of seals. For information about boat fishing, enquire at Berwick harbour.
Shilbottle: Contact boatman. Tel: 01665 575731.

BEACHES

Alnmouth
Wide stretch of sand at low tide; bathing is not advised because of very strong currents.

Bamburgh and Seahouses
Fine stretches of sandy beach with rocky outcrops. No dogs on the small beach at Seahouses. Only safe to bathe on incoming tides because of strong currents.

Beadnell Bay
Sands curve 2 miles (3.2km) south from Beadnell. Restrictions on dogs on part of beach, (look for signs), because of nesting birds.

Druridge Bay
Sands, dunes and grassland.

Embleton Bay
Wide, dune-fringed beach. Bathe only when tide is coming in.

Spittal
Popular sandy beach at the mouth of the Tweed.

Warkworth
Three miles (4.8km) of wide, firm sands, backed by dunes to the north of Warkworth. Do not bathe at high tide.

BOAT TRIPS

Amble
Round Coquet Island in summer, weather permitting. Contact Puffin Cruises. Tel: 01665 711975, or enquire at Amble Tourist Information Centre.

Seahouses
To the Farne Islands, weather permitting – from Seahouses

harbour. Contact boatmen. Tel: 01665 720308, 720825 or 720388 – they all have permission to land on Inner Farne or Staple; also round trips without landing.

COUNTRY PARKS, FORESTS AND NATURE RESERVES

Amble Dunes Nature Reserve.
Budle Bay Nature Reserve, Bamburgh.
Cresswell Pond Nature Reserve, Amble.
Druridge Bay Country Park, Amble.
Hauxley Nature Reserve.
Lindisfarne Nature Reserve, Holy Island.
Scotch Gill Wood Nature Reserve, Morpeth.
Thrunton Wood, near Callay.

CYCLE HIRE

Bamburgh
Mountain Bike Hire, 34 Front Street. Tel: 01668 214535.

Berwick-upon-Tweed
Brilliant Bikes, 17a Bridge Street. Tel: 01289 331476.

Ford/Etal
Brilliant Bikes, Heatherslaw Corn Mill. Tel: 01890 820338.

Morpeth
Cycleways, 54 Newgate Street. Tel: 01670 515153.

GOLF COURSES

Alnwick
Alnwick Golf Club, Swansfield Park. Tel: 01665 602632.

Alnmouth
Alnmouth Golf Club. Tel: 01665 830231.

Bamburgh Castle
Bamburgh Castle Golf Club. Tel: 01668 214378.

Belford
Belford Golf Club, South Road. Tel: 01668 213433.

Berwick-upon-Tweed
Goswick Golf Club. Tel: 01289 387256.
Magdalene Fields Golf Club. Tel: 01289 306384.

Embleton
Dunstanburgh Castle Golf Club. Tel: 01665 576562.

Warkworth
Warkworth Golf Club, The Links. Tel: 01665 711596.

GOLF DRIVING RANGES

Belford
Belford Golf Club, South Road. Tel: 01668 213433.

HORSE-RIDING

Alnwick
Windy Edge Stables, Alnmouth Road. Tel: 01665 602284.

Cornhill-on-Tweed
Whitehouse Riding School, Cornhill House. Tel: 01890 882422.

Haggerston
Haggerston Stables, Chapel House. Tel: 01289 381237.

Kimmerston
Riding Centre, Milfield, Wooler. Tel: 01668 216283.

Morpeth
Benridge Riding Centre. Tel: 01670 518507.

Seahouses
Slate Hall Riding Centre, South Lane. Tel: 01665 720320.

LONG-DISTANCE FOOTPATHS

The Northumberland Coast Walk
A 25-mile (40.2km) walk from Alnmouth to Budle.

The Northumbrian Coastline
A 61-mile (98.2km) walk from Berwick to North Shields.

Annual Events and Customs

Alnwick
Shrove Tuesday Football Match
Alnwick Fair, late June–early July.
International Music Festival, early August.

Berwick-upon-Tweed
Riding the Bounds, early May.
Allerdean Country Fair, May Day Bank Holiday.
May Fair, last Friday in May.
Military Tattoo, early September.
Running the Walls, early September.

Morpeth
Northumbrian Gathering, weekend after Easter.

Tweedmouth
Tweedmouth Feast, late July.

The Hills

Turbulent history and a sense of remoteness set the hills of
Northumberland apart. These high, windswept moors
and deep valleys were once bitterly fought
over by English and Scots. Protection
came from fortified bastle houses and pele
towers. Now there is peace – though the
army makes its presence felt – and much of
the area is protected as National Park.

'It is the land of the far horizons, where the
shapes of gathered vapour are for ever moving along the furthest ridges of
the hills, like the procession of long primeval ages that is written in tribal
mounds and Roman camps and Border towers, on the breast of
Northumberland', wrote G M Trevelyan of his native county.

ALWINTON   Northumberland Map ref NT9106
The small village of Alwinton in the Upper Coquet
Valley is set between the grassy Cheviots and the more
rugged Harbottle Hills, and makes a good base for
exploring. Sir Walter Scott found it a good base, too,

*Windy Gyle, not far from
Alwinton and Harbottle, is
one of many good places
for walking in the area*

AT HOME ON THE RANGE

Access to 58,000 acres of the Northumberland hills is restricted by its use for military exercises. Each year 30,000 troops come here for weapons training and air-to-ground attack practice. Northwest of Otterburn is the live firing area. Red flags or lamps warn when roads and footpaths are shut – always obey them. On open days, stick to the paths and don't pick anything up. The area north of the River Coquet has no live firing, but blanks and flashes are used. Roads and paths here are always open, but the same rules apply, and don't be surprised if you meet camouflaged soldiers on manoeuvres. Local Tourist Information Centres have details of firing times and copies of public access guide.

THE PACK AND THE SPUR

A 700-year-old grave slab in Bellingham churchyard is called the Long Pack; legend says that it marks the tomb of a robber who in 1723 was brought into a local house rolled in a pedlar's pack, so that he could secretly open the door to his accomplice. Servants became suspicious when the pack wriggled, and one of them discharged a shotgun at it. A shriek and blood revealed the dying man.

At nearby Hesleyside Hall is kept a large Tudor spur. The Charlton Lady of the Manor would produce it at supper from under a dish cover when she found that her supplies were running down, as a sign that the men should set off for Scotland for a spot of raiding to replenish them. Her action is shown in a painting in the Central Hall at Wallington.

staying at the popular Rose and Thistle while he was researching his heroic tale, *Rob Roy*.

Alwinton church is away from the village, on the hillside south of the river, and from its large churchyard there are wonderful views. Each October the village hosts the last of the season's traditional shows – the Border Shepherds' Show – with sheep, fell racing and sheepdog trials.

Nearby Harbottle, another pleasant village, has a jolly memorial fountain and the remains of the de Umfraville's castle. The 30-foot (9m) Drake Stone, high on the hillside, is reputedly a black magic site, while Holystone Burn Wood, a nature reserve, has birch, juniper and oak woodland.

At Chew Green, 8 miles (12.8km) west of Alwinton, is one of Britain's best Roman earthworks. The remains of a fort and camp are clearly visible among the hills and you can reach the site from Redesdale when the army firing ranges are not in use – a drive with superb views along the Roman Dere Street.

BELLINGHAM   Northumberland Map ref NY8383

The body of St Cuthbert, on its 100-year wanderings from Lindisfarne to Durham, was an early visitor to Bellingham (pronounced 'Bellin-jum'), the capital of North Tyne. Cuddy's Well, named after him, was said to have miraculous properties and is used for baptisms in St Cuthbert's Church, a fascinating early 13th-century building. The church was rebuilt in the early 17th century, when it was given its remarkable stone-vaulted roof, probably to protect it from fire in the frequent Scots' raids. Cannon balls were found in the roof when it was restored.

Outside Bellingham's Town Hall is more evidence of warfare – a gun captured at the Boxer Rebellion in China in 1900 – and the presence of army training areas is felt here today. For ten years from 1838 the town was a thriving iron and coal centre, but the industry was killed by competition from foundries nearer Newcastle upon Tyne and on Teesside. The evidence of that activity remains, though, in the cottages built for the workers along the banks of Hareshaw Burn, and grassed spoil heaps can be seen on the path up to Hareshaw Linn waterfall at the head of its fine wooded gorge (see Walk on page 44).

Bellingham, which hosts a famous agricultural show in August that features pig racing, is an excellent base for exploring the Northumberland National Park and the Kielder area. About 7 miles (11.3km) northwest of Bellingham, remote in the Tarset Burn valley, is Black Middens Bastle, one of very few which are open to the public. About 200 of these defensive stone houses were built by wealthy farmers in the 16th century in order to protect their families and livestock, and Black Middens Bastle is a typical example. Bastles were usually about

35 feet (10.7m) by 25 feet (7.6m) in area, with two storeys. The beasts occupied the windowless ground floor and the people reached the upper floor by a removable ladder – the stone stairway at Black Middens was a later addition.

BRINKBURN PRIORY Northumberland Map ref NU1298

Brinkburn Priory is beautiful, and is picturesquely set among beechwoods in a narrow valley beside the River Coquet. Augustinian Canons lived here from about 1130 until Henry VIII's Dissolution of the Monasteries. The roof of the great church fell during the 17th century, but the estate owner restored it in the mid 19th century – unusually for those days, his architect rebuilt exactly what was here around 1200.

A cross-shaped building with a low central tower, it has perfect proportions and round-headed Norman windows, just turning pointed Gothic in places. The interior is mostly empty, in true medieval style. Very little remains of the rest of the monastic buildings – just a few walls which were built into the Georgian house south of the church.

MONKS AND SMUGGLERS

The best of the ancient green routes for walking in Northumberland is Clennell Street from Alwinton to Yetholm, which has been used for many purposes over the centuries. Ancient settlements along the way indicate that it may have been a prehistoric route across the hills, but unlike Dere Street, equally ancient, it was never made into a Roman road. It continued to be used into the Middle Ages – in 1181 monks from Newminster called it 'the great road of Yarnspath' as they visited their sheep-runs on the hills; drovers used it in the 18th century, while in the 19th smugglers brought whisky from illicit stills, such as Rory's Still on the Usway Burn high in the hills. It is a good route (in fine weather) to the Scottish border and to Russell's Cairn on Windy Gyle, a superb viewpoint to the Eildon Hills in Scotland and across the Cheviots.

The Gothic priory church of Brinkburn was carefully restored by Thomas Austin in the 19th century

To Hareshaw Linn and Back

Linn is the Northumbrian name for a waterfall and, exciting though the whole walk is, the most impressive sight (and sound) is saved for the very last moment when water bursts forth over a shadowy rock face in a bower of trees high overhead. It is mostly easy walking, but there are some ups and downs; paths are mainly good and some sections are paved.

Time: 2 hours. Distance: 2½ miles (4km).
Location: Bellingham is in the North Tyne valley, 18 miles (29km) northwest of Hexham on the B6320.
Start: From the town centre take the road signposted 'Redesmouth' and in 50 yards (45.7m) turn left opposite the Police Station. The Northumberland National Park car park is 200 yards (182.9m) along this lane beside the Hareshaw Burn. (OS grid ref: NY840835.)
OS Map: Outdoor Leisure 42 (Keilder Water) 1:25,000.
See Key to Walks on page 121.

series of impressive waterfalls, cascades and deep pools that are typical of a hill burn. Just above the falls there is a second bridge, followed by a third where the gorge becomes narrower and steeper. After the fourth and fifth bridges, the gorge becomes narrower still, with huge boulders littering the burn, which have fallen from the steep rock walls above.

A wooden walkway along a steep bank leads to stone steps and then to the sixth and final bridge, where the roar of the Linn can be heard. Through a glade the first glimpse appears, but when you climb up the steps the Linn comes into full view. A path passes under a huge overhang to allow a closer look at the tumbling water, but an arc of vertical rock wall prevents any further progress. Retrace your steps to return to the car park by the same route.

ROUTE DIRECTIONS

The path heads upstream from the car park on the left of the fence, then goes on through the farm gate, or kissing gate, and past Foundry Farm. Walk uphill to the next kissing gate. At an open area, bear right and continue up the path through an area of small hillocks which were once the spoil heaps of the local iron industry. At the edge of the wood a kissing gate leads on to a paved path, gradually gaining height before arriving, after 800 yards (732m), at the first bridge over Hareshaw Burn.

A short distance upstream from this point is the first of a

The woodland around the Hareshaw Burn and waterfall supports a rich diversity of plantlife, including interesting ferns and mosses

POINTS OF INTEREST

Hareshaw Ironworks

Hareshaw was a hive of industrial activity in the 1840s. Both iron ore and coal were mined here and many spoil heaps are still in evidence, even though they have now been reclaimed by nature. Part of a dam, built to provide water power for the furnace bellows, still exists above Foundry Yard. Competition from other ironworks, nearer to the big towns and railways, sounded the foundry's death knell and it closed in 1848. Ironically, the railway came to the town in 1862, passing right by the yard, but it was too late to save the ironworks – and now the railway too has gone.

Hareshaw Dene

Now managed and owned and by Northumberland National Park Authority, there is unrestricted public access to both the Dene and the Linn. They have been popular with visitors for more than a century and the six bridges spanning the burn were originally constructed by the people of the town.

Wildlife of the Linn

Wild flowers are abundant along the Linn, with primroses everywhere in the woods in spring, marsh marigolds along the burn and the meadows blue with harebells in the late summer. In the autumn a wide variety of woodland fungi flourishes among the fallen leaves.

The deep sheltered Dene is a haven for wildlife too. Dippers and grey wagtails nest along the burn, and the woodland birds include redstart, wood warblers and pied flycatchers. Roe deer

Look out for the flickering flight of the pied flycatcher, just one of the woodland birds which can bee seen in the area

may occasionally be seen, especially early or late in the day, and there is at least one badger sett.

Hareshaw Linn Project

In 1999 the local community, working in close association with the Northumberland National Park Authority, began work on the project to improve the path and bridges in Hareshaw Linn.

The strange little church at Elsdon huddles behind a low wall

THE HUNTING OF THE CHEVIOT

Of all the Border Ballads *Chevy Chase* is perhaps the most famous. Earl Percy goes hunting in the Cheviot 'With fifteen hundred bowmen bold' and is challenged by the Scots Earl Douglas with 'Full twenty hundred Scottish speres'. Battle is joined and the earls fight until they have 'blood downe their cheekes like raine'. Neither will yield, but an English arrow kills Douglas. Percy pays tribute to his noble foe – 'a more redoubted knight mischance could never take' – but is killed himself by Hugh Montgomery, whose 'hatfull spere' goes through Percy's body 'a large cloth-yard or more'. After the battle 'scarce fifty-five' Scots and 'but fifty-three' English are left.

ELSDON Northumberland Map ref NY9393

Elsdon by the River Rede was the capital of the remote Middle March – one of three set up in 1249 for protection along the border. The large and attractive triangular green, surrounded by mainly 18th- and 19th-century houses – look for the figure of Bacchus on a former inn – was once used to pen up the stock during attacks. From the early 12th century the village was guarded by Elsdon Castle, built on the Mote Hills to the north by the de Umfravilles. It lasted only until 1160, when they moved to Harbottle Castle. The motte and bailey earthworks remain, though, the best in Northumbria.

The 14th-century Elsdon Tower – a defensive pele for Elsdon's vicars – stands near the church. Rebuilt in the 16th and 18th centuries, it gives a strong impression of the dangers of Scots raids. The church, another St Cuthbert's, said to be one of the places where his body rested during his wanderings, is isolated on the green. Its bell-turret dates from 1720, but most of the building is from the 14th century. The inside is odd, with very narrow aisles and thick walls – probably also for defence. More than 1,000 skulls, and other bones, were found here in the 19th century – bodies of soldiers who fell at the Battle of Otterburn in 1388. And in 1877 a box with three horse skulls was found in the little spire. No one knows how they came to be there.

INGRAM Northumberland Map ref NU0115

The narrow Breamish Valley is one of the joys of the National Park, and Ingram, sited on the Park border, is a fine gateway to it. The small village church (with its large Georgian rectory) is more interesting inside than its frowning exterior might suggest – bits of it may be pre-Norman – but most visitors come to Ingram for the scenery. To help them, the National Park Authority has access agreements with landowners, and there are car parks and picnic sites along the valley both east and west of the village. There is excellent walking from the village right up to the Scottish border – and beyond. There are Iron-Age hillforts and deserted medieval villages in the valley, too – look out for the earthworks as you walk, especially if the sun is low. Linhope Spout, 3 miles (4.8km) west of Ingram, is one of the county's best waterfalls, reached by a path from Linhope beside the river.

KIELDER Northumberland Map ref NY6293

Kielder Water is the largest man-made lake in Europe, 9 miles (14.5km) long and holding 41 million gallons of water. Size and majesty go together here, too, with the huge Kielder Forest – the largest wooded area in Britain – coming down to the shore. At the west end is the dam, finished in 1982, which is three-quarters of a mile (1.2km) long, complete with valve tower, and gives an idea of the scale of the undertaking. Facilities for visitors are generous, too. Tower Knowe Visitor Centre on the southern shore is a mine of information, and you can sail the water on the ferry from here. There is also an exhibition about the area's history, as well as shops, eating places and picnic sites – as there are at Leaplish Waterside Park and at Kielder Castle Visitor Centre at the northwest end. The castle was the 18th-century shooting box of the Dukes of Northumberland. You can drive the 12 miles (19.3km) from Kielder to Byrness along the Forest Drive – there is a toll to pay, but it is well worth it for the experience. And all around the water and in the forest there are opportunities for fishing, sailing, windsurfing, riding, mountain-biking, orienteering and walking along well-signed tracks.

PEDAL POWER

Even the least adventurous can enjoy cycling at Kielder. Bring your own bike or hire one, either from the north end of the dam from Leaplish Waterside Park or from Kielder Castle. You can choose from several types, depending on whether you want rugged mountain cycling or a more gentle route along bridleways and roads. From the dam, a popular route, suitable for families with children from about eight upwards, is along the North Haul Road to Kielder Castle. Setting out from the castle, you can follow the old road and the former railway track to Deadwater Station, on the Scottish border, or for a little more adventure, have a go at cycle orienteering on the Archercleugh Trail Quest. With the help of a map, find cut-outs of animals hidden in the forest, punch your card and see how quickly you can complete the trail.

Kielder Water, on the edge of the Northumberland National Park, has provided a new focus for leisure activities in the area

Kielder – a Spectacular Man-Made Landscape

A walk in the heart of Kielder to see the size of the reservoir and the scale of woodland planting, as well as some of the plant and birdlife of the area. The forest tracks and paths are very boggy in places, so waterproof footwear is vital at all times. Orange waymarkers help you find the latter part of the route.

Time: 2¼ hours. Distance: 3 miles (4.8km).
Location: 20 miles (32km) northwest of Hexham.
Start: In Bull Crag car park on the south side of Kielder Water.
(OS grid ref: NY676865.)
OS Map: Outdoor Leisure 42 (Kielder Water)
1:25,000.
See Key to Walks on page 121.

ROUTE DIRECTIONS

Walk back along the track that you drove along to reach the car park. At the road turn right, and walk by a sign 'Otterstone Viewpoint'. Walk along the track and turn left at the second viewpoint sign

The work of the Forestry Commission has changed the face of Kielder in recent years

into an open area. Go to the right of a stone wall, through a gate towards the stand of Scots pine.

Beyond the pines is the **Jubilee Plantation**. Pass a stone seat and at an information board walk towards the water to meet a crossing path. Turn right towards a fence and over a stile. Cross a burn and go through a gap in a stone wall. Follow the signs keeping straight on through the **woodland**. At a crossing track turn left towards the water and then turn right to follow the **former main road** for about a quarter of a mile (400m). As the tarmac ends, go right along a signed path, eventually through woodland, and back to the edge of the lake. From here

there is a good view of the dam.

Go along the path round the end of the headland and back into the woodland. At a T-junction turn right up a track, climbing slightly. At the top of the second rise, take a track to the left. The path descends to the water's edge and winds through trees. Whickhope Cruiser Centre can be seen across the water. Pass over a wooden bridge, go round the head of a small inlet, down steps and across a second wooden bridge. Cross a track and return to the car park ahead and the start of the walk.

POINTS OF INTEREST

Kielder Forest, Kielder Water and Dam
Kielder Forest, part of the Border Forest Park, is Britain's largest single wooded area. Together with Kielder Water, it offers a wide variety of recreational activities, including riding, walking, mountain-biking and sailing. The Visitor Centre at Tower Knowe will tell you what is available and explain the history of the flooded valley.
The dam at the eastern end of the water is three quarters of a mile (1.2km) long and 169 feet (52m) high, and was built between 1975 and 1981. The building which stands alone in the water is the valve tower. The largest man-made lake in Europe, Kielder Water covers more than 2,600 acres, is 9 miles (14.4km) long and can hold more than 41 million gallons of water.

Jubilee Plantation
The enclosed plantation of pines was planted overlooking the reservoir in 1977 to commemorate the Silver Jubilee of the

accession to the throne of Queen Elizabeth II.

Woodland

Much of the woodland at Kielder is Sitka and Norway spruce, which grow rapidly in this climate and produce wood that can be used both for pulp and for building. Norway spruce, which has grown up to 138 feet (42m) in Britain, is the traditional Christmas tree, and its cones have scales with wavy ends. Sitka spruce grows more quickly, with a British record height of 164 feet (50m). Its cone scales have rounded ends.

On the fringes of the woodland several different bird species may be glimpsed, including the redpoll and coal tit. The crossbill, Britain's only bird with a beak that is specially adapted to open cone scales to extract the seeds, is sometimes to be seen, and you may hear the great spotted woodpecker tapping its beak on dead boughs. In some places along the walk you may see bird boxes, which have been supplied by the Forestry Commission for birds like the tawny owl,

whose natural nesting places in old trees have been removed by forest management.

The Former Main Road

Before the dam was built and the valley flooded, this was part of the main road through the North Tyne Valley. The metalled surface, with its white lines along the centre, is gradually succumbing to time and nature.

The wide expanse of Kielder Water is popular with watersports enthusiasts

You can't go far in the National Park without seeing its flying curlew sign. The whaup, as it's known locally, is one of the birds most likely to be seen – or at least heard – on the moorland in the spring and summer. With its distinctive 5-inch (13cm) bill, brown speckled plumage and white rump, it is the largest of Britain's waders. Its 'coor-li' song (hence its name) is heard throughout the year, and in spring, when the male performs its courtship display over the moorland, it has another, trilling call. The females lay three or four eggs in nests on the moorland in April or May.

Military skills of a bygone age can be tested at Otterburn Hall

THE NORTHUMBERLAND NATIONAL PARK

Some of the remotest parts of Northumberland form the 398 square miles (1,030sq km) of the Northumberland National Park, which also takes in some of the best stretches of Hadrian's Wall. It attracts more than a million visitors each year, but has a resident population of only around 2,500. National Park status recognises its special value to the whole nation, but doesn't change the ownership of the land – three-fifths is owned privately, mostly by farmers who struggle to make a living in the difficult uplands. You can't just wander at will in the Park, but the National Park Authority negotiates access agreements for the public, runs visitor centres, organises walks and publishes guides and leaflets. It also supports the local farmers, offering grants for conservation purposes, such as mending stone walls and managing traditional woodland, and also helps them to deal with the pressures that even the most careful visitors inevitably cause.

Another fifth of the Park consists of the Forestry Commission's extensive conifer plantations, but more controversial is ownership of the remaining 20 per cent. The Ministry of Defence was here long before the National Park was designated in 1956, but many consider its training areas inconsistent with National Park status.

OTTERBURN   Northumberland Map ref NY8893

Otterburn has always had its place in military history, since the famous Battle of Otterburn, on 19 August 1388, brought together Harry Hotspur, son of the Earl of Northumberland, and Earl Douglas, who commanded a Scots raiding party. Versions of the battle – and opinions

about where it happened – vary, but agree that it was fought by moonlight, that the Scots beat Hotspur in a daring manoeuvre, that Douglas was killed and Hotspur captured, to be ransomed later. Many of the dead were buried at Elsdon church. The Percy Cross, in a plantation northwest of the village, is traditionally where Douglas died. Today's soldiers practise live firing on the Otterburn Training Area to the north: on certain days there is public access along rights of way and roads – check locally for dates, and don't stray. At Otterburn Mill, originally built in the 18th century, you can buy fine tweeds and woollens, while Otterburn Hall, a YMCA hotel, has 85 acres of grounds with forest walks, nature trails, donkeys and sheep, and activities such as archery and canoeing.

ROTHBURY   Northumberland Map ref NU0501/NU0803
One of the main tourist centres of Northumberland, Rothbury, the capital of Coquetdale, is an attractive town, with stone buildings spreading outwards from an irregularly shaped green and a medieval bridge over the River Coquet.

The town suffered from William Wallace's army in the 13th century, and proclaimed the Old Pretender as James III in the 18th, but since the 19th century it has developed as a holiday centre.

FOREST WALKS
Harwood Forest, on the Simonside Hills southwest of Rothbury, is managed by the Forestry Commission, which has laid out waymarked walks of different grades, all starting from their car park near Great Tosson. A one-mile (1.6km) lower-level walk gives glimpses of the Coquet and the Cheviots, and there are two more adventurous routes, one climbing Ravens Heugh Crags, with wide views and the chance to see grouse and blackcock on the moorland, and one going to the 1,411-foot (429m) summit of Simonside, with spectacular views of hills and coast.

The superb gardens at Cragside include around 40 miles (64.4km) of scenic drives and footpaths

THE MODERN MAGICIAN
William Armstrong, born in Newcastle in 1810, began his scientific career while fishing on the Coquet. He became interested in hydraulics after watching an inefficient waterwheel, and went on to found his engineering works at Elswick on the Tyne to make hydraulic cranes and lifts. After the Crimean War he invented the breech-loaded Armstrong Gun, and armour plating for warships. Despite his great fortune and peerage he remained a quiet and humble man, still fishing the Coquet with his old friends and continuing to experiment and invent, giving Cragside not only lamps made by his friend the electrical pioneer Swan, but also hydraulic lifts and kitchen spit, telephones between the rooms and electric gongs. Cragside was the first house in the world to be lit entirely by electric light and visitors can see the lakes that fed the hydro-electric plant in the Power House and the ingenious timber flume, canal and pipeway that brought water to them on their hillside site.

The parish church suffers from its Victorian restoration, which destroyed a Saxon tower and left very little of the rest, but it is worth visiting to see the font – its bowl dates from 1664, but stands on part of the 9th-century Rothbury Cross, decorated with vigorous Celtic-inspired designs.

East of Rothbury the Coquet rushes through a narrow gorge at The Thrum – you can reach it by a footpath from the bridge. In places no more than 5 feet (1.5m) wide, the river has scoured the sandstone here into contorted shapes; it has also been harnessed to provide power for Thrum Mill's undershot waterwheel. West of Rothbury, near the tiny and picturesque village of Holystone, is the atmospheric Lady's Well, a stone-lined pool amid trees, where St Paulinus is said – probably wrongly – to have converted and baptised 3,000 locals in AD 627. An 18th-century statue of the saint stands beside the well.

Cragside (National Trust), east of Rothbury, is one of Northumberland's major tourist attractions and can be very busy in high season, but with more than 900 acres of country park and gardens, it is usually easy to find a quiet corner. Built for the 1st Lord Armstrong by architect Norman Shaw, it is a fantastic Victorian creation, a cross between an English manor house and a Bavarian schloss. It hangs over the gorge of the Debdon Burn in a sea of trees and its interior is full of heavy late-Victorian atmosphere, though parts are dark, cramped and rather disappointing. Spectacular exceptions include the fine library and the drawing room, with its huge alabaster fireplace.

WALLINGTON Northumberland Map ref NZ0284
Wallington is a place of history and historians. A medieval castle here was owned by the Fenwicks until 1684 – the last was Sir John, executed for plotting to assassinate William III; his horse, White Sorrel, was taken by the king, who was thrown and killed after it stumbled over a mole hill. Parts of the castle survive in the cellars of the present plain, square house, built in 1688 and altered around 1745. These changes transformed the

A charming detail of the fine plasterwork adorning the library at Wallington

A view over Wallington's splendid walled garden

inside with a new grand staircase and wonderfully delicate plasterwork, most elaborate in the high Saloon, where Reynolds' portrait of Sir Walter hangs, and wall cabinets display part of Wallington's famous china collection. There is fine Chippendale and Sheraton furniture, 18th-century needlework and a fascinating collection of dolls' houses.

The Trevelyans were at Wallington for almost 200 years and one of them married the sister of historian Lord Macaulay, whose library is now here. Macaulay's great nephew was another historian, George Macaulay Trevelyan; it was his brother who gave Wallington to the National Trust in 1941.

Wallington shone brightest in the 19th century, when Sir Walter Trevelyan and his wife Pauline entertained writers, scientists and artists – Swinburne, the poet from nearby Capheaton, and the painter Millais among them. It was at Ruskin's suggestion that the courtyard was roofed, creating an Italianate central hall with two levels of open arches. Murals of Northumbrian history by William Bell Scott include *The Descent of the Danes*, with Pauline as a woman crying during a Danish raid, and *The Building of Hadrian's Wall*, with Newcastle's town clerk as a centurion, but best of all is *Iron and Steel*, showing the modern industries of Newcastle.

The stables are almost as grand as the house, with a big central clocktower originally designed as a chapel. The grounds include a beautiful walled garden with a little pavilion and terrace overlooking lawns and an ornamental stream with banks of flowers – one of the prettiest gardens the National Trust owns.

THE GARDENER'S BOY

The best-known English gardener, Lancelot 'Capability' Brown was born at Kirkharle, 1½ miles (2.4km) from Wallington, and went to school at nearby Cambo. At 16 he was gardener's boy at Kirkharle Tower and was soon designing a new layout for part of the grounds. His fame spread to other local estates, and in 1739 he moved south, becoming head gardener at Stowe by 1741. His practice grew swiftly, and he designed gardens all over the country, swiftly sizing up their 'capabilities' and producing designs using trees, water and grass as the main elements. Appointed Master Gardener at Hampton Court in 1764, he had a hand in most of the major country house estates in the 18th century.

Forest Tracks and Fine Views

A walk along the sandstone fells of Rothbury Terraces, with wide views of the beautiful Coquet Valley and the Simonside Hills, as well as a glimpse of the Cragside Estate and a chance to visit the popular small town of Rothbury. The going is good, with mostly level walking on tracks and clear paths, though there are some muddy and boggy stretches across the open moorland, and a stiff climb at the start.

Time: 2½ hours. Distance: 5 miles (8km).
Location: 11 miles (17.6km) miles south-west of Alnwick.
Start: In the centre of Rothbury. Park on or near High Street.
(OS grid ref: NU057017.)
OS Maps: Explorer 332 (Alnwick & Amble) 1:25,000.
Outdoor Leisure 16 (The Cheviot Hills) 1:25,000
See Key to Walks on page 121.

ROUTE DIRECTIONS

From the green in the centre of **Rothbury** take the narrow passage, **The Nick**, to the right of the Co-op supermarket, opposite the telephone kiosk. Turn left at the top, and after a few yards turn right up a footpath signed 'Hillside Road ¼ mile'.

At Hillside Road turn right and then first left, up a road signed 'Cartington 2¼'. As the road bends left by houses, continue straight ahead between two fences to a stile. Continue along immediately by the edge of a conifer plantation and uphill to meet a crossing path.

Turn left towards a television mast to pass a cairn and join a track. Follow it for 1½ miles (2.4km) as it winds along **Rothbury Terraces**. Pass a plantation on the right and as the track bends to the right the remains of **Old Rothbury** can be seen below. This section of the track has wide views of the

Simonside Hills and the **Coquet Valley**. Continue along the track now heading north, with views of the Cheviots.

Ignore crossing tracks and head towards a plantation. The track goes parallel with the plantation wall and curves into woodland. Go ahead through two gates and follow the track for three quarters of a mile (1.2km) around the edge of Primrose Wood, through a gate and descend to a gate by Primrose Cottage. Turn right through a second gate up into Primrose Wood.

At the sign 'Rothbury 1¼' turn left. Follow the track through woodland. Just after the second track joins from the right, turn left along a waymarked path to a stile. Follow the path over the moorland. To the left is the edge of the **Cragside** Estate. Pass a stone carved with R and D, and climb up the ridge, passing a stile, to reach

a crossing track at a waymark sign. Continue ahead on to the original path back to Rothbury.

POINTS OF INTEREST

Rothbury and The Coquet Valley
A busy tourist town, Rothbury retains its Northumbrian character. The parish church holds part of the 9th-century Rothbury Cross, supporting the font, with carvings of humans and animals in ferocious struggle. As the River Coquet (rhymes with 'soak-it') passes Rothbury it is squeezed between the hills to rush through The Thrum, a narrow, wooded ravine where the sandstone has been worn into fantastic shapes by the action of the water.

The Nick
This narrow pathway is on the route of pilgrims visiting St Helen's Well near Cartington, claimed to have healing powers. Helena, reputed to have discovered the True Cross in Jerusalem in AD 335, was the mother of the first Christian Emperor, Constantine, and may have visited Northumbria with her husband, Emperor Constantius Chlorus.

Rothbury Terraces
The reddish sandstone fell is scored here into parallel lines by the action of glaciers. The moorland is covered with heather, bracken and bilberry, and among the birds that may be seen are curlew, redshank, golden plover, sandpipers and kestrels.

Old Rothbury
The Iron-Age hill fort was built to guard the Coquet Valley. Constructed and

Looking out over Rothbury to the jagged line of the Simonside Hills

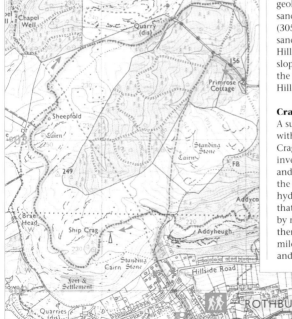

occupied between about 550 BC and AD 43, the grassed remains consist of a double ditch and the outline of the stone foundations of hut circles.

The Simonside Hills

A huge river system in geological times deposited sand more than 1,000 feet (305m) deep that forms the sandstone of the Simonside Hills. There are steep scarp slopes and imposing crags; the highest peak, Tosson Hill, is 1,444 feet (440m).

Cragside

A superb Victorian house with rich period interiors, Cragside was built for the inventor Lord Armstrong, and was the first house in the world to be lit by hydro-electricity. The lakes that fed it are surrounded by millions of trees, and there are more than 40 miles (64km) of footpaths and drives.

A ROYAL GARTER
In Northumberland's other
Wark – 7 miles (11.3km)
northwest of Kirknewton – is a
castle which was once an
important border fortress but
is now very ruined. Edward III
is said to have founded The
Order of The Garter here in
about 1348. It was at a ball,
after the king had again
defeated the Scots, that the
Countess of Salisbury dropped
her garter. The king, to
prevent his courtiers mocking
her, fastened it on his own
leg, with the words 'Evil to
him who thinks evil of it'. The
motto – in French *Honi soit qui
mal y pense* – is still
embroidered in gold on the
insignia of the Knights of the
Garter.

WARK Northumberland Map ref NY8677

Wark used to be a place where Scottish kings held their
court, the capital of the Regality of Tynedale, once
guarded by a motte and bailey castle. After the Earl of
Derwentwater's disgrace for supporting the Old
Pretender's 1715 rebellion, the parish, with its
neighbours, was given to Greenwich Hospital, which put
naval chaplains in as rectors. They all had similar
churches and rectories, too. Don't be misled by Wark's
untidy look from the main road; turn towards the river
to find a green surrounded by stone houses.

Over the bridge, the road leads to Chipchase Castle, a
mix of medieval pele, Jacobean manor and Georgian
interiors above the North Tyne Valley. The Heron
family, 'Keepers of Tynedale', were often at odds with
their neighbours, so the 14th-century building's walls,
9 feet (2.7m) thick, the portcullis (which still remains)
and the corner turrets were useful defences. Cuthbert
Heron joined a new house on to the old tower in the
17th century, but in 1727 the family had to sell, and
eventually Chipchase came to John Reed, who added
sash windows throughout – even on the ancient tower –
and gave the inside elegant plaster ceilings and good
furniture and china. The gardens are worth visiting too,
with wild and vegetable plots, as well as a lake.

The huge Wark Forest, west of the village, is the largest
wooded area in Northumberland National Park, and is
home to roe deer and red squirrels. There are waymarked
forest trails from Stonehaugh, where the picnic site is
famous for its collection of totem poles.

St Mungo's Church in the attractive village of
Simonburn, 2½ miles (4km) south of Wark, once served
the whole area from Hadrian's Wall to the Scottish
border – the largest parish in England. Despite that, it is
disappointingly over-restored. Much better is the Old
Rectory, mostly built in 1725 and looking rather like an
elegant 18th-century mill.

*Chipchase Castle is a
pleasing mansion dating
from 1621, built around a
much older defensive tower*

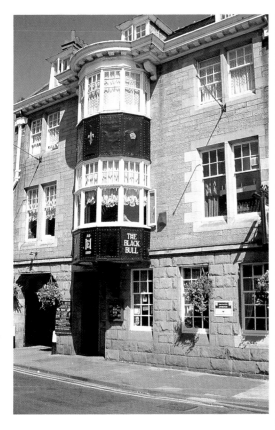

The old market town of Wooler suffered disastrous fires in the 18th and mid-19th centuries, so many of the buildings post-date that time

WOOLER Northumberland Map ref NT9927

Wooler's attractions lie on its doorstep rather than in the town itself, though it is a pleasant, work-a-day place, full of local farmers and visiting walkers and fishermen. It is often called 'Windy Wooler', and few of its buildings have much grandeur, but with the great Cheviot massif immediately to the west and south of the town, it is the hills that attract most visitors. There is evidence of early settlements all over the area, and the Battle Stone beside the A697 to the north of the town is a reminder of the fighting between the Scots and the English at Humbleton Hill.

To the south of the town are the beautifully wooded Happy Valley and the Harthope Valley, which was formed by the Harthope Burn, flowing through a fault in the hills. You can drive through Earle and the delightfully named Skirl Naked as far as Langleeford, where Sir Walter Scott came for the fishing. From here it is walking country – to the summit of the Cheviot (it is boggy and disappointing when you get there) or, from further down the valley, through the hills and around Yeavering Bell.

FORTRESS AND PALACE

It is worth the climb up to the 1,182-foot (360m) summit of Yeavering Bell to see both the view and the remains of Northumberland's most spectacular Iron-Age fortress, with its massive rubble wall that was once 10 feet (3m) thick – part of it has been reconstructed to show what it was like. More than 130 timber buildings – the largest 42 feet (13m) across, occupied the 13½-acre site. Below the hill was King Edwin's palace, Ad Gefrin, mentioned by Bede and discovered by excavation in the 1950s – a monument by the road marks the place. St Paulinus baptised local people in the River Glen to the north in AD 627, and probably preached in Ad Gefrin's most unusual feature, a wooden theatre like an open-air university lecture hall.

The Rolling Hills of Humbleton

A walk among the magnificent Cheviot Hills, with hill forts, battle sites and medieval fortifications as well as views of the sea. Paths and tracks are through high moorland, with a steep track near the start. There are some boggy places and you should not attempt this walk in poor visibility.

Time: 4 hours. Distance: 6¾ miles (10.8km).
Location: 15 miles (24.1km) south of Berwick-upon-Tweed.
Start: High Humbleton, northwest of Wooler. Park carefully on the roadside near the telephone kiosk, or near the ruined cottage just up the rough track near a gate.
(OS grid ref: NT976285.)
OS Map: Outdoor Leisure 16 (The Cheviot Hills) 1:25,000.
See Key to Walks on page 121.

ROUTE DIRECTIONS

Walk up the track, go through a gate and go straight ahead, climbing to a second gate, with **Humbleton Hill** to the right. Beyond a third gate bear right uphill as the track divides. Follow 'St Cuthbert's Way' signs from here. The route climbs as the track winds round to the right, and on through a gate. There are views of the sea to the right. Follow the signed path beneath the summit of Gains Law. It bends left alongside a broken wall and diagonally left up a path at a waymarker. Continue along the marked path and on to a grassy track, turning left.

After half a mile (800m) go through a waymarked gate in the wall on the right and follow the path left over a stile and alongside the wall. There are fine views of Iron-Age hillfort **Yeavering Bell** to the right. Near a gate in the wall,
turn right along the marked path and pass by a small cairn to reach a track. Turn right and follow the track round to the left, through a gate and alongside a plantation, turning right at the corner. Go through a gate and follow the track through another gate beyond the corner of a further plantation, then eventually descend steeply to a gate near a farmhouse.

Beyond the gate veer right along the grassy track that winds over a small bridge.

Follow the track and just before a gate turn right to a stile and follow the wall up the slope, turning left at the corner of the wall. Go through a gate and follow the path alongside the wall and round the hillside. As the path bends right, the nearest building in Akeld is a **Bastle House**. The path climbs the hillside to reach a stile beside a gate.

Go over the stile, alongside the wall then straight ahead across the field and downhill to a ladder stile. Cross a small burn and follow the signed path to a hand gate. Follow the wall beyond, passing a **duck pond** and then bearing right through two gateways to reach the ruined cottage.

POINTS OF INTEREST

Humbleton Hill
Scene 1 of Shakespeare's *Henry IV* gives news of the Battle of Holmedon (or Homildon), where the English army met 10,000 Scots. Here, on 14 September 1402, 'they did spend a sad and bloody hour'. The Scots occupied Humbleton Hill, easy targets

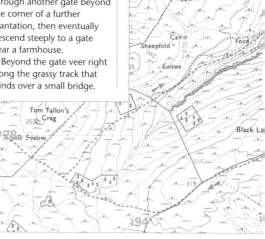

for the English archers on Monday Cleugh to the west – so many arrows were fired that the Scots looked like hedgehogs. The Scots fled after heavy fighting below the hill, especially in a field known as Red Riggs, which ran with blood. A prehistoric standing stone 6½ feet (2m) high beside the road is now known as the Battle Stone. The Iron-Age fort on top of Humbleton Hill is still partly encircled by the remains of walls up to 10 feet (3m) wide.

Yeavering Bell

The best of Northumbria's Iron-Age hill forts, the summit of Yeavering Bell is still surrounded with a massive rubble wall, once 10 feet (3m) thick. Within its 13½ acres was a small town made up of circular timber huts. At the foot of the hill

was Ad Gefrin, palace of King Edwin – St Paulinus stayed here in AD 627 – and of King Oswald.

Akeld Bastle House

The solitary stone building nearest to the foot of the hill is a Bastle House, one of more than 200 in Northumberland built by farmers to protect themselves and their stock from border raiders. Described in 1541 as 'a lytle fortelett or castle house' the lower floor was for the

The Cheviot Hills provide excellent walking country, rich in historic associations

animals and the upper, originally reached by ladder through a hole little more than 1 foot (30cm) square, was for the farmers.

Duck Pond

This small pond has been formed by damming the sike to create a habitat for ducks, where they could be shot for the table from hides along the edge.

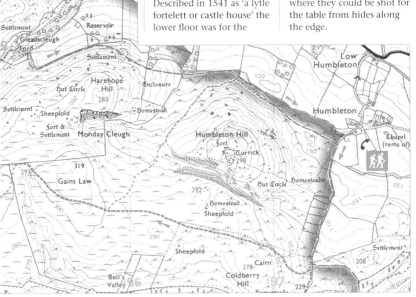

The Hills

Checklist

Leisure Information

Places of Interest

Shopping

Sports, Activities and
the Outdoors

Annual Events and Customs

Leisure Information

TOURIST INFORMATION CENTRES

Bellingham
Main Street.
Tel: 01434 220616.
Rothbury
National Park Visitor Centre.
Tel: 01669 620887 (seasonal).
Wooler
Market Place. Tel: 01668
282123 (seasonal).

NORTHUMBERLAND NATIONAL PARK CENTRES

Northumberland National Park Headquarters
Eastburn, South Park, Hexham.
Tel: 01434 605555.
www.nnpa.org.uk
Ingram
Visitor Centre. Tel: 01665
578248 (seasonal).
Rothbury
Church House, Church Street
Tel: 01669 620887 (seasonal).
Northumbrian Water Visitor Centre
Tower Knowe, Kielder Water.
Tel: 01434 240398.

NATIONAL PARK INFORMATION POINTS

Cambo
Cambo Post Office. Tel: 01670
774217.

Elsdon
Impromptu Café. Tel: 01830
520389.
Falstone
Falstone Tea Rooms. Tel: 01434
240459.
Harbottle
Cognet Crafts. Tel: 01669
650348.
Milfield
Milfield Country Store & Café.
Tel: 01668 216535.
Otterburn
The Border Reiver, Main Road.
Tel: 01830 520682.
Wooler
Brands, 43 High Street.
Tel: 01668 281413.

OTHER INFORMATION

Regional Tourist Information
www.visitnorthumbria.com
English Heritage
Tel: 0870 333 1181
www.english-heritage.org.uk
National Trust for Northumbria
Scots' Gap, Morpeth.
Northumberland. Tel: 01670
774691.
www.nationaltrust.org.uk
Northumberland Wildlife Trust
Garden House, St Nicholas Park,
Jubilee Road, Newcastle upon
Tyne. Tel: 0191 284 6884.

www.wildlifetrust.org.uk/
northumberland
Northumbria Water
Abbey Road, Pity Me, Durham.
Tel: 0191 383 2222.
www.nwl.co.uk
Otterburn Ranges
Information from Range Control
Tel: 0191 239 4261.

ORDNANCE SURVEY MAPS

Landranger 1:50,000 Sheets 74,
75, 80, 81, 87, 88.
Outdoor Leisure 1:25,000
16 (The Cheviot Hills),
42 (Kielder Water)

Places of Interest

There will be an admission
charge at the following places
of interest unless otherwise
stated.
Black Middens Bastle House
Bellingham. Open any
reasonable time. Free.
Brinkburn Priory
Longframlington. Tel: 01665
570628. Open Apr–Oct daily.
Chipchase Castle
Wark. Tel: 01434 605270.
Open: garden Apr–Jul, certain
days, castle open June.
Cragside
Rothbury. Tel: 01669 620333.
Open: house Apr–Oct most
afternoons; gardens and

grounds Apr to mid-Dec, most days.

Kirknewton College Valley
Permits to drive beyond Hethpool in advance (personal callers or SAE) from Sale and Partners, 18-20 Glendale Road, Wooler. Tel: 01668 281611. Open throughout the year, except lambing season (mid-Apr to end May). Free.

Wallington House Walled Garden and Grounds
Cambo. Tel: 01670 774283. Open: house Apr–Oct most afternoons; walled garden and grounds all year daily.

SPECIAL INTEREST FOR CHILDREN

The following places may be of interest to visitors with children. Unless otherwise stated, there will be an admission charge.

Keilder Water Bird of Prey Centre
Leaplish, Keilder. Tel: 01434 250400.

Otterburn Hall (YMCA)
Otterburn. Tel: 01830 520663. Attractions include forest walks, nature trails, donkeys, pony and sheep. Open all year daily. Free.

Shopping

LOCAL SPECIALITIES

Crafts and Gifts
The Border Reiver, Otterburn. Tel: 01830 520682. Craft gallery, coffee house and shop.

Pottery
Westfield Farm Pottery and Gallery, Thropton, Rothbury. Tel: 01669 640263.

Textiles
Otterburn Mill. Tel: 01830 520225. Knitwear, tweeds and rugs.

Sports, Activities and the Outdoors

ANGLING

Fly
Kielder Water: Kielder Water Visitor Centre. Tel: 01434 240398. Permits are available from the machines at the lodge by the dam, at Leaplish Waterside Park and Bakethin

Weir Car Park.
North Tyne River: Permits are available from the Black Cock Inn, Falstone. Tel: 01434 240200.

BOAT HIRE

The Reivers of Tarset Centre for Watersports. Tel: 01434 250203.

BOAT TRIPS

Kielder Water Cruises. Tel: 01424 240398. Easter–October, daily from Tower Knowe or Leaplish. Evening Cruises, July–August. Telephone in advance.

CYCLE HIRE

Kielder
Northumbrian Water Cycle Hire, Leaplish Waterside Park, Leaplish. Tel: 01434 250312. Keilder Bikes, Keilder Castle. Tel: 01434 250392.

Rothbury
The Spar Shop, High Street. Tel: 01669 621338.

Wooler
Haugh Head Garage. Tel: 01668 281316.

GOLF COURSES

Bellingham
Bellingham Golf Club, Boggle Hole Farm. Tel: 01434 220530.

Rothbury
Rothbury Golf Club, Old Race Course. Tel: 01669 621271.

Wooler
Wooler Golf Club, Dod Law, Doddington. Tel: 01668 281137.

HORSE-RIDING

Kielder
Calvert Trust, Kielder Water. Tel: 01434 250232.

Otterburn
Redesdale Riding Centre, Soppitt Farm. Tel: 01830 520276.

Rothbury
Whitton Farmhouse Hotel. Tel: 01669 620811.

COUNTRY PARKS, FORESTS AND NATURE RESERVES

Harwood Forest, near Rothbury. Holystone Burn Wood Nature Reserve, near Alwinton. Harthope Valley, near Wooler.

ORIENTEERING

Kielder
Information from Kielder Castle. Tel: 01434 250209.

WATERSPORTS

Kielder Water
Information from Northumbrian Water, Leaplish. Tel: 01434 250312.
The Reivers of Tarset Centre. Tel: 01434 250203.

Annual Events and Customs

Alwinton
Border Shepherds' Show, mid-October.

Bellingham
Bellingham Show, late August.

Falstone
Border Shepherds' Show, mid-August.

Rochester
Upper Redesdale Show, late September.

Rothbury
Traditional Music Festival, mid-July.

Whalton
Baal Fire, early July.

Wooler
Glendale Show, late August.

Sheepdog trials are a feature of local agricultural shows in summer

Along Hadrian's Wall

From Wallsend near the mouth of the Tyne to Bowness on the Solway Firth, Hadrian's Wall swept across the North, 'to separate', the Emperor's Roman biographer wrote, 'the Romans from the barbarians'. Much of the wall – a World Heritage Site – and its forts can still be traced, often in remote countryside. It provides a sense of the history of Britain, which later fortifications and the handful of towns along its most impressive sections enhance. The finest stretches of Hadrian's Wall are built on the dramatic dolorite outcrops of the Great Whin Sill, formed 295 million years ago when molten rock forced its way through the earth's crust. This chapter is arranged geographically, east to west, rather than alphabetically.

BUILDING THE WALL

Although Hadrian ordered the wall, it was built under the supervision of Nepos, Governor of Britain. It took eight years and the work was done by soldiers from three legions – the 2nd, based in Caerleon; the 6th, in York; and the 20th, in Chester. They had expert engineers, surveyors, masons and carpenters – some may have helped to build turf and timber walls in Germany. As work progressed, other soldiers, including auxiliaries, helped, and there may have been locally conscripted labour, too. The cost would have largely been accounted for by the soldiers' normal pay – indeed, it is suggested that the wall was built partly to occupy them.

THE WALL

Around AD 80 the Romans constructed a road – Stanegate – south of the Whin Sill. It went from Corbridge, where Dere Street crossed the Tyne, to Carlisle. Guarded by forts, it was not originally a frontier, for Roman troops were active far into Scotland. But in about AD 100 Emperor Trajan withdrew to the Stanegate, building new forts and watch towers on the Whin Sill. Trajan's successor, Hadrian, visiting in AD 122, ordered the construction of a permanent wall.

Running 80 Roman miles – 73 modern miles (117.5km) – the wall was built of local sandstone between the Tyne and the Irthing; further west turf was used, later replaced by stone. It began 10 Roman feet – 9½ feet (3m) – wide, later reduced to 8 feet (2.4m), or sometimes 6 feet (1.8m), to speed up the construction. The vallum, a high-banked ditch south of the wall to control civilians at the frontier, was another modification.

No one knows exactly how high the wall was – probably around 21 feet (6.4m). For some of its life it was whitewashed. There were regular crossing points, for the wall was never meant to be an impenetrable barrier. Instead, it gave the Romans control over journeys in the area. The barbarians could pass into the Empire, but only to approved markets, unarmed and with a military escort. Later, in more troubled times, some of the gates were blocked.

When Hadrian died in AD 138, the new Emperor, Antoninus Pius, abandoned the wall, pushed into Scotland and built the Antonine Wall (of turf rather than stone) from the Forth to the Clyde. But the troops retreated to the Whin Sill in the 160s, when a new route – the Military Way – was built between the wall and the vallum to improve access.

The tribes north of the wall were kept in check much of the time, though occasionally there were rebellious outbreaks. By the beginning of the 4th century there was a new menace – the Picts – and successive Emperors tried to deal with them. The Empire was breaking up by AD 407, when the British army chose its own Emperor, Constantine III, who went to win Rome, leaving Britain undefended. The auxiliaries at the wall drifted away, and it became a quarry for local farmers. Hadrian's part in the Wall's construction was forgotten until 1840, and it has only been in the 20th century that it has gained legal protection.

The line of Hadrian's Wall stretches away across the hills from Twice Brewed – some of the best remaining sections are to be seen on the southern fringe of the National Park

Aydon Castle is an important example of a medieval fortified manor house

Unlike the great forts at Housesteads and Chesters, *Onnum*, also known as Halton Chesters, half a mile (800m) north of Halton, is virtually unvisited. The wall here is hidden under the Military Road, and the northern part of the fort, beyond it, has long been ploughed over. But it was an important place, garrisoned by 500 soldiers, including cavalry – it is the only place where evidence of stables has been found on the wall. Built after about AD 124, when forts were built on, rather than near, the wall, it was abandoned while the Romans were in Scotland in the 2nd century, re-garrisoned later and then finally deserted in the late 4th century. You can still trace its outline on the ground south of the road, and muse on mortality.

AYDON CASTLE Northumberland Map ref NY9966
Set in a curve of the Cor Burn just north of Corbridge, Aydon Castle, recently restored by English Heritage, is really a very early fortified manor house, built at the end of the 13th century and given its battlements in 1305. Where it was most vulnerable, to the north side, it has an irregular outer bailey, and behind that a small, open courtyard, with the living quarters to one side. Unusually for its early date, there was no keep. Instead there was a hall and a solar with a fine fireplace and beautifully detailed windows – don't miss the bearded face staring out from above the northern one. Look out, too, for the garderobes – medieval toilets – at the southeast corner of the strong south range. Within the walls there was an orchard, so that conditions must have been comfortable for this unsettled border country. Despite this it had its excitement, being captured by the Scots in 1315, and by English rebels in 1317. In the less fraught 17th century it became a farmhouse – which helped to preserve its main features.

At Halton, three quarters of a mile (1.2km) north, you can get a glimpse of Halton Tower (not open), a 14th-century pele with a wing of 1696, and visit the chapel next door. This may be Saxon in origin – it was certainly here in Norman times – and has a wonderfully simple interior, its white-painted walls contrasting with the massive wooden beams of the roof.

CORBRIDGE Northumberland Map ref NY9964

The first Roman fort at Corbridge – *Corstopitum* – was built around AD 90, more than 30 years before Hadrian's Wall, to guard the bridge where Dere Street crossed the Tyne. The Stanegate, built slightly earlier by Agricola's troops, also crosses the fort on its way to Carlisle. As an important junction, *Corstopitum* had a succession of forts – the one we see today is the fourth, built about AD 140 as the Romans occupied Scotland. It was an important military headquarters, depot and supply base, even after the Romans gave up on Scotland towards the end of the 2nd century. By degrees it changed into a town – the most northerly in the Roman Empire – much of which is still buried, though its stones are found in many Corbridge and Hexham buildings.

The excellent museum is full of finds from the site, including inscriptions and small, often personal objects. The recommended visit takes you first past the granaries, perhaps the most memorable part of the fort, and the best preserved in Britain, with floors of stone slabs on low walls.

The square courtyard to the north of the main street (part of Stanegate) was never finished and no one is quite sure what it was. Opposite are the military compounds, where you can trace the workshops and officers' houses, descend into the former strong-room and see where the soldiers and locals worshipped both Roman and local gods.

The town, once Northumbria's capital, suffered badly from invasion by Danes and Scots. Not surprisingly, there are two defensive pele towers in Corbridge. One, at the end of Main Street, dates from the 13th century and was converted into a comfortable house in about 1675.

FOUNTAIN LION

Pride of place in the museum at *Corstopitum* goes to the Corbridge Lion. A finely carved, spirited beast with a bushy mane, it is depicted, mouth open, attacking a stag. It is thought that the lion started life on a tomb, but was later moved to ornament the great fountain in the town. You can still see the fountain's large stone tank, which was fed by an aqueduct, between the granaries and the courtyard building. The tank's edges were worn down by centuries of metal blades being sharpened against the stone.

The remains of the granaries at Corbridge's Roman fort are particularly impressive

MILECASTLES, TURRETS AND FORTS

At every Roman mile along the wall was a milecastle, like a tiny fort. It had a gate in its southern wall, and one to the north through the wall itself, so that travellers could be checked as they passed through it. Most milecastles had barracks for eight men – though a couple of them held 32. Between each milecastle were two look-out turrets. There may have been a walkway along the top of the wall. By the time the wall was finished there were also 12 forts between Wallsend and Carlisle, each with at least 500 soldiers, so the full complement manning the wall was around 10,000. Most of the forts were 14 Roman miles – a day's march – apart, so that any border trouble could be dealt with swiftly.

SAXON SEAT

In the chancel of Hexham Abbey is one of its treasures, the stone chair called Wilfrid's Seat or the Frith Stool – frith means sanctuary, and those who sat on it claimed the protection of the Church. Dating from the time St Wilfrid built the church, the chair had a place of honour in the Saxon building, and is ornamented with plait and knot patterns. The great crack that splits across it was due not to violence or natural disaster, but to Victorian workmen who dropped it in 1860.

Hexham's abbey includes an intriguing mixture of monuments and memorials, including an Anglo-Saxon cross and Roman altars

The other, the Vicar's Pele, is built of Roman stones and was probably put up in the 14th century. Set in the churchyard and little altered over the centuries, it is one of the best peles in the north.

St Andrew's Church, too, uses Roman stones – between tower and nave is a whole Roman archway. The tower's lower parts were probably built before AD 786, and there is more Saxon work in the walls, as well as a Norman doorway and a fine 13th-century chancel. Lots of stone cross slabs are built into the walls and floors, and part of the chancel floor is a medieval altar stone, continuing the area's recycling traditions.

HEXHAM Northumberland Map ref NY9364

St Etheldreda gave the manor of Hexham to her spiritual adviser, Wilfrid, for supporting her against her husband King Egfrith. Wilfrid built the first priory – it was never an abbey – in about AD 674. His biography, written about AD 700, describes 'the very deep foundations, the crypts of beautifully-finished stone, the great building supported by different columns, walls of wonderful height and length. We have never heard of anything like it this side of the Alps'. Wilfrid's crypt, reached from the new nave built in 1907, was built of Roman stones from *Corstopitum* (see Corbridge, page 65), many still with carvings or inscriptions, and the 7th-century plasterwork is still rock-hard.

The rest of the priory is impressive, too, especially the

early 13th-century choir, the north transept with fine lancet windows and, in the south transept, the Night Stair for the Augustinian canons to descend from their long-vanished dormitory for night prayers. Look out for the nearby Roman tombstone of standard-bearer Flavius, shown riding a fat pony over a hairy barbarian. The stalls in the choir have carved misericords, while Prior Leschman's Chantry contains spirited carvings of unlikely subjects like a bagpiper, a fox preaching to geese and a lady combing her hair.

The priory was set apart from the town by a row of houses towards the market place, with its stone-columned Shambles, still used by traders. The Riot Act was read here in 1761 to lead-miners protesting against conscription. Be sure to make time to visit the 14th-century Moot Hall, a miniature castle with an archway tunnelling through it, which now houses the Border Library and Gallery. Through the arch, in Hallgate, is another fearsome tower, the Archbishops' Gaol. Built about 1330, it houses the Border History Museum.

Hexham is a good town to stroll around, with some stunning Victorian shop-fronts and fine houses. The street names, too, have a particular charm – St Mary's Chare and Priestpopple, for example. Tyne Green is a riverside country park and Hexham Race Course is south of the town.

Hexham is set in attractive rolling Border country

CENTRING ON THE ARTS

Hexham has an annual music festival based at the priory, but for year-round entertainment, the enterprising Queen's Hall Arts Centre opposite is the place to go. Housed in the former town hall (and looking like a French *mairie*), the centre has an intimate 400-seat theatre, with a constant programme of professional and amateur theatre, music and other events; a public library; a gallery and studio, both showing a wide variety of changing exhibitions; and a good restaurant. Not surprisingly, it is a popular focus for both local people and visitors.

Three Dales

A spectacular 70-mile (112.7-km) drive that takes you to the valleys of the Tyne, Wear and Tees and across some of England's wildest and most remote moorland. Much of the route is within the officially designated North Pennines Area of Outstanding Natural Beauty. Note: Some of the route passes over unfenced, high moorland. You should not attempt this drive in bad weather or when visibility is low.

ROUTE DIRECTIONS

See Key to Car Tours on page 120.
From the centre of Hexham take the B6305 west towards Allendale turning left at the traffic lights by the Fox Inn. Follow the main road, signed 'Allendale', to Catton. Go through Allendale Town, with its attractive square surrounded by stone houses

and continue down the valley of the River East Allen for 7½ miles (12.1km) through Sinderhope, with its precariously perched chapel, into Allenheads, once an important lead-mining centre. 1½ miles (2.4km) beyond the village cross the County Durham border and descend into Weardale.

The B6295 joins the A689 just before Cowshill. At the junction you can turn right for 2½ miles (4km) to visit **Killhope Wheel and the Lead Mining Centre**. On the main route, turn left to go through Cowshill and Ireshopeburn and into the centre of St John's Chapel, with its 18th-century church and the only Town Hall in a Durham village. Turn right up a narrow entry, Harthope Road, signed 'Langdon Beck'. The unclassified road eventually goes over a cattle grid and climbs steeply on to Harthope Moor. This is one of the highest public roads in England, attaining an altitude of 2,057 feet (627m). The road is marked by tall poles, indicating the route when covered by snow. Do not attempt this route in bad weather or limited visibility. Follow the road for 5 miles (8km), to descend, with wide views of the valley, into Teesdale.

At the junction with the B6277 turn left, signed 'Langdon Beck, Middleton'. After half a mile (0.8km) a road right leads to Cow Green Reservoir and Cauldron Snout. Continue along the B6277 for 3 miles (4.8km) to reach the spectacular High Force water-fall. In 1½ miles (2.4km) is **Bowlees Visitor Centre**,

Derwent Reservoir offers a range of attractions, including a nature reserve and a country park

and then the road enters the former lead-mining centre, Middleton-in-Teesdale.

Immediately after crossing the bridge into Middleton turn sharp left, up a steep hill signed 'Stanhope'. After half a mile (800m) turn right, again signed 'Stanhope'. After 4½ miles (7.2km) pass over a cattle grid, round a sharp right-hand bend and turn left and left again on to the B6278. The road goes over moorland with spectacular views for 8½ miles (13.7km), to descend into Weardale. Just before the river the road bends left and then right over a bridge to join the A689.

Turn right into the centre of Stanhope and turn left, signed 'B6278 Edmundbyers', just beside the Grey Bull public house. Go up the steep hill through Crawleyside and after 2½ miles (4km), where the main road goes slightly right, continue ahead on an unclassified road, signed 'Blanchland'. Follow this road for 5½ miles (8.8km) across open moorland and descend into the valley of Beldon Burn at Baybridge. Go over the bridge, back into Northumberland, and follow the road into Blanchland.

In the village take the road straight ahead beside the abbey tower, signed 'Hexham, Corbridge'. As the road ascends there are views over Derwent Reservoir. The road passes through Slaley Forest and descends to the very narrow Linnels Bridge over Devil's Water, and 2 miles (3.2km) further reaches the centre of Hexham.

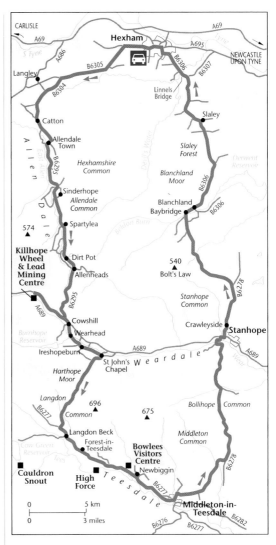

Rusted wagon wheels at Killhope recall its days as an important lead-mining centre

The main chambers of the Roman bath house can still be identified at Chesters

CLAYTON'S COLLECTION
Without John Clayton (1792–1890) there would be much less of Hadrian's Wall. As well as owning and landscaping the Chesters estate and fort, he bought long stretches of the wall and several of the other forts, including Housesteads (see page 72). He was active as an archaeologist, laying open to view many Roman remains, and collecting objects from them. The fascinating museum at Chesters is a memorial to him. Among its treasures are statues of a reclining river god, from the commanding officer's bath house, and the (now headless) goddess Juno Dolichena. Notice, too, the corn-measure from *Carvoran* which erred generously towards the Romans.

CHESTERS Northumberland Map ref NY9170
Where Hadrian's Wall crossed the North Tyne, the Romans built a wooden bridge guarded by *Cilurnum* fort, now called Chesters. Cavalry were stationed here – no remains of stables have been positively identified, but we can see the barrack-block where the soldiers lived in groups of eight. The officers had larger rooms, at the river end of the block. In the centre of the fort was the headquarters, where the commanding officer sat on a raised platform to dispense justice. The rooms behind were used by regimental clerks and the standard-bearers, who also looked after the accounts and pay. A stone staircase leads into the vaulted strong-room, which still had its iron-sheathed oak door when excavated in the early 19th century. Both the well-preserved east gate and the west gate have short sections of the wall attached.

Near the river was the garrison's bath house. We can still trace its main chambers – the changing room, with niches probably for clothes, the hot dry room, like a sauna, hot steam rooms, hot and cold baths, as well as the latrine, draining to the river. Furnaces and under-floor heating must have made this one of the most desirable places in the camp.

Near by are remains of the bridge, but they are better preserved on the opposite bank – reached by a footpath from the bridge at Chollerford. In the river you can see an original pier, which carried the wooden pedestrians' bridge to the first of its ten supports, as well as its successor of about AD 206. This new bridge carried vehicles and was all of stone; two of its three piers can be seen when the river is low.

CARRAWBURGH Northumberland Map ref NY8771
Brocolitia, the fort at Carrawburgh, remains largely
unexcavated, though it is known that it was an
afterthought to the wall, added in around AD 130. The
vallum alongside the wall had to be filled in before the
fort could be built, and, unlike earlier forts, it did not
project north of the wall.

Near by are the remains of the most complete Mithraic
Temple found in Britain. Originally an Eastern religion
that told of the struggle between light and dark,
Mithraism was the most popular religion along the wall,
rivalling Christianity, which had by this time become
the official religion of Rome. The temple was low and
dark, representing the cave where Mithras slew the
primeval bull and in doing so brought innumerable
benefits to mankind. The uninitiated gathered in a small
ante-room. Beyond this was the temple, with three altars
(those you see today are replicas) and statues of Mithras's
attendants, Cautes, torch raised to represent light, and
Cautopates, torch down for darkness.

One of the altars shows Mithras as the Unconquered
Sun. Above the altars there was once a sculpture of
Mithras and the Bull – perhaps destroyed by Christians
during the 4th century. The seven Mithraic grades of
worshippers – Father, Courier of the Sun, Persian, Lion,
Soldier, Bridegroom and Raven – would sit or kneel on
low wattle and wooden platforms as the mysteries,
which included a symbolic meal of bread and water,
took place.

The original altars, and other artefacts, can be seen in
the Museum of Antiquities in Newcastle upon Tyne;
there is also a full-scale reconstruction of the temple,
highly coloured as it was once.

BRITANNIA DESOLATA
Coventina's Well, a powerful
spring beside the fort, was
dedicated to a Celtic water
goddess, whom the Romans
were happy to include in their
beliefs. Protected by a shrine,
the spring attracted votive
coin-throwers – more than
16,000 coins were excavated
in 1876, mostly small change,
but with some silver and gold,
too, as well as other objects,
including a bronze model of a
Scottie dog. There were brass
coins, too, struck when the
Emperor Augustus Pius put
down the North after local
rebellion in AD 155; they show
defeated Britannia with
bowed head and lowered
banner, the picture of
submission.

*The reconstructed Mithraic
temple in Newcastle's
Museum of Antiquities
attempts to capture the
atmosphere of the original
at Carrawburgh*

ROMANS AND RAILWAYS

Did George Stephenson study Roman cart tracks at Housesteads' East Gate? It was once the fort's main entrance, but one of its two arches was soon blocked, and the guardroom used as a coalhouse. So the other side took all the traffic, and over the centuries the passage of carts wore grooves in its stone threshold. They are 4 feet 8½ inches (1.4m) apart – standard railway gauge today, thanks, at least in part, to Stephenson, who came from Wylam only 20 miles (32km) away. Alas for romance, the East Gate was still unexcavated in Stephenson's day. But the link remains, for farm carts retained this axle span when he began his engineering career. Despite Brunel's attempts at 8-foot gauge, Stephenson's building on traditions more than 1,500 years old won the day.

HOUSESTEADS Northumberland Map ref NY7869

Housesteads – Roman *Vercovicium* – is the most visited fort on Hadrian's Wall because of its spectacular site, impressive remains and access to one of the best parts of the wall. Consequently it can be crowded at summer weekends.

To get an idea of the main features, and see some of its treasures, visit the museum first, then climb to the remains of town buildings by the South Gate. These buildings may have been shops or taverns – they still show the grooves that once held shutters. The gate itself was rebuilt as a bastle in the Middle Ages for a family of horse-thieves. Through it, to the right, visit the communal latrines, where 12 soldiers could sit, rinsing their cleansing sponges in the water channels.

Housesteads followed the usual fort pattern, with the headquarters in the centre and the commanding officer's house south of it. You can also see the remains of the hospital, complete with operating theatre, and the granaries. The North Gate has huge foundations on the crag above Knag Burn – the fort protected this vulnerable point. A classic wall view is from the northeast corner of the fort, over the burn.

Walk the wall westwards from Housesteads to Milecastle 37 – the views are wonderful – and on, if you can, to Steel Rigg, worth the effort to see how the fearsome military structures of Rome have been absorbed into the Northumbrian landscape.

Roman latrines sufficient for a whole garrison can be seen at Housesteads

VINDOLANDA Northumberland Map ref NY7867

Agricola had a turf fort at *Vindolanda* in the AD 80s to guard the Stanegate, and part of the paved road, as well as a Roman milestone, can still be seen here. Another fort was built before Hadrian's time, and when the wall was put up, the fort was rebuilt in stone, then almost totally rebuilt 100 years later, with its usual rectangular shape. The layout of the headquarters and parts of the gates are visible.

Vindolanda also has the biggest civilian settlement to be seen on the wall. Visit the *mansio* (an inn for travellers) with its bath house, and the large 'corridor' house, part of which was a butcher's shop. Other buildings, long, thin 'strip houses', had their narrow ends to the street to avoid high taxes. The town bath house was used by women and children as well as men – hairpins and a child's sandal were found in the drains. You can still see some of the pink waterproof plaster that lined the walls and floors.

Children visiting *Vindolanda* make straight for the reconstructions of sections of Hadrian's Wall, based on archaeological evidence. The Turf Wall shows what the original, Cumbrian, part of the wall was like – it was soon rebuilt in stone. Here it has a timber gateway, as may have been found at the milecastles. More impressive is the Stone Wall, nearly 23 feet (7m) high, with battlements, turret and ditch.

Vindolanda's waterlogged soil preserved many trivial details of daily life – the museum shows some of them, including leather shoes, textiles and ornaments. There is also a replica of a Roman kitchen. Most important are the wooden writing tablets, with gossip, party invitations, letters requesting new underwear, and accounts of food stores, bringing the Romans and their neighbours vividly to life.

The timber milecastle at **Vindolanda** *helps bring the soldiers' story to life*

FROM A ROMAN KITCHEN

A popular Roman recipe – spiced cabbage:

1 small green cabbage, 2–3 leeks, 1 tablespoon white wine, 1 tablespoon oil, 1 teaspoon caraway seeds, ¼ teaspoon ground cumin, 1 teaspoon of liquamen*.

Shred, boil and strain the vegetables. Mix the other ingredients, heat and pour over the vegetables.

*Liquamen, used in many Roman recipes, contained: ½ glass red wine, ½ pint (30cl) water, 3oz (75g) salt, 2–3 anchovies or brisling. These were mixed, boiled for ten minutes and strained into bottles.

A RAILWAY NAME?

Haltwhistle's intriguing name might suggest a link with the railway – indeed, this was once an important junction on the main east–west line to Carlisle, where passengers could change for a scenic Pennine route to Alston, long since closed. But the name has been around much longer. It was Hautwisel in 1240, and seems to mean 'the place where the streams meet by the hill' – although other suggestions are 'the high place by the crescent of water' and 'high boundary'. All of them seem to fit with Haltwhistle's geography.

Haltwhistle's church of golden stone is a good example of Early English architecture

HALTWHISTLE Northumberland Map ref NY7064

Haltwhistle Burn flows into the South Tyne east of the town of Haltwhistle, and there are pleasant walks alongside the burn up to Hadrian's Wall. Haltwhistle is also a good place from which to explore the north Pennines. But don't neglect the attractive town centre, its stone streets radiating from the market place giving it a slightly stern, Scottish air. Some of its Victorian station buildings, including the stationmaster's house, waiting room and ticket office, date from as early as 1838. The Red Lion Inn is based on a defensive tower, probably of the 17th century, when Haltwhistle was still at the mercy of Scottish raiders. It was under the protection of the powerful Ridley family (still big landowners in Northumbria); the tomb of John Ridley, brother-in-law to Nicholas Ridley, the Protestant martyr burned at the stake in 1555, is in Holy Cross Church.

The church is one of Northumberland's best, at least on the inside – its exterior is rather unprepossessing, though the setting is pleasant. It is mostly Early English, with long, thin lancet windows, and was carefully restored in 1870, when the wonderful stained glass, by William Morris's company, was put in the east windows. Haltwhistle was once a thriving industrial centre (there are still manufacturing plants in and around the town), and by the burn you can see the remains of woollen mills, collieries, brickworks and lime kilns.

Great Chesters fort – *Aesica* – is 2 miles (3.2km) north and was built around AD 128, after the wall, to guard the Caw Gap. Not much is left, though a blocked gateway can be seen, and you can trace the remains of an aqueduct that supplied the fort with water.

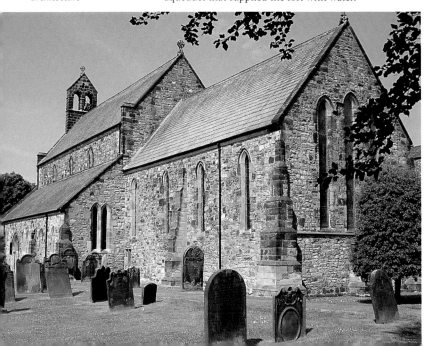

CARVORAN Northumberland Map ref NY6667
Magnis fort at *Carvoran* was built before Hadrian's Wall,
to guard the junction of the Stanegate and the Maiden
Way, running from the South Tyne to the Eden Valley in
Cumbria. You can still make out the main shape, but the
only stones visible are part of the northwest tower.
Adjoining the fort is the exciting Roman Army Museum,
with finds from *Magnis* and other sites along the wall,
and a large-scale model of the fort. Push-button displays
provide instant access to specific details, so that visitors
can select what interests them. Here, too, the life of the
soldier on the wall is brought to life, with full-size figures
showing the uniform, armour and weapons for the
legionaries and auxiliaries. Find out how much they
were paid, what they ate, how they were trained – and
how they overcame boredom at the edge of the Empire.

East of *Carvoran,* the wall runs over the Nine Nicks of
Thirlwall, once nine gaps in the Whin Sill, reduced to
five by quarrying. Turret 45A was probably a signal post
in use while the wall was being built – its stones are not
keyed into the structure. To the west, there is a fine
stretch of the vallum, and beyond it the 14th-century
Thirlwall Castle, beside the Tipalt Burn. Built, as usual,
against the Scots, where there was a gap in the wall, it
played host to Edward I on 1306, but was largely derelict
by 1542. The last recorded inhabitants left in the 18th
century, although a dwarf ghost is supposed to remain,
guarding a gold table.

QUIS CUSTODIET?
Hadrian's Wall wasn't guarded
by shivering Italian
legionaries, but mostly by
auxiliary troops, recruited
from Britain or elsewhere in
the northern Empire. They
were divided into mixed
infantry and cavalry regiments
of 500 men, though there
were some of 1,000. Their
officers were often
inexperienced aristocrats,
serving briefly before
returning to civilian life.
Infantry units were divided
into centuries – oddly, with 80
men – and cavalry into troops
of 32, led by professional
soldiers – one centurion is
known to have served 58
years. They spent their time
patrolling the wall or training.
They were not allowed to
marry, but often had unofficial
liaisons in the civilian towns at
the fort walls.

*Soldiers of the Ermine Street
Guard bring a breath of
'living history' to Roman
sites along the wall*

Roman Wall and Medieval Castle

A usually quiet and always interesting stretch of Hadrian's Wall, and a medieval castle, are highlights of this varied walk. Waterproof footwear is needed at all times; crossing the Tipalt Burn on stepping stones needs care, and should not be attempted after heavy rain. An alternative, shorter route goes through Low Old Shield, missing out Thirlwall Castle and crossing the vallum.

Time: 2½ hours. Distance: 4 miles (6.4km).
Location: 15 miles (24.1km) west of Hexham.
Start: In the National Park car park at Walltown, northwest of Haltwhistle. (OS grid ref: NY668659.)
OS Map: Outdoor Leisure 43 (Hadrian's Wall)
1:25,000.
See Key to Walks on page 121.

ROUTE DIRECTIONS

From the car park, follow the Pennine Way eastwards alongside the road for half a mile (800m), over a cattle grid. At a footpath sign 'Walltown Crags' turn left towards **Hadrian's Wall**. On reaching the wall, the route goes right, but a short diversion left gives good views towards the Cumbrian hills. Returning to the wall, follow it along the top of **Walltown Crags**, past **Turret 45A** and descend into the valley north of Walltown Farm and turn left along a track.

Follow the track as it bends left and then right, go through a gateway and diagonally left past a waymark sign towards the roofs of High Old Shield. Go over a ladder stile in the wall, downhill across a footbridge and turn left on the metalled track. Turn right up the entrance to High Old Shield, signed 'Cairny Croft ¾'. Where the track bends left, go over two stiles, follow the waymarked route behind the farm to go over another stile.

Follow the stone wall and then descend to a stile. Cross another field, go over a stile in a stone wall and turn left. Follow a track to a further

At Walltown the wall's builders made full use of natural landscape features

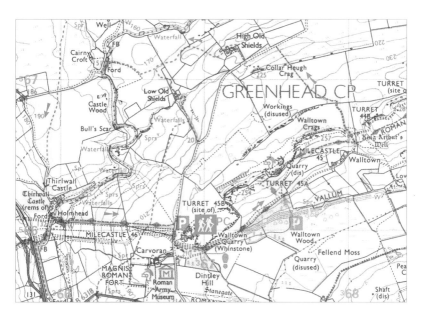

stile, and walk left of a wooden hut to a footpath sign. (To avoid the crossing of the burn, turn left towards Low Old Shield to join the metalled track in half a mile/800m, turning right to the car park.) For the full route, continue straight ahead, then make towards the white cottage in the valley. Descend to cross a stile beside the burn, turn left and go over the stepping stones.

Follow the road uphill for a quarter of a mile (400m) to a footpath sign in the fence on the left. Go over the stile, cross the field to another stile, and go diagonally to a gate in the corner of the next field. On the road turn left and descend to **Thirlwall Castle**. Take the farm track to the right of the castle, go over a footbridge and along the track by the buildings. After a right-hand bend, turn left up a track beyond a single stone gatepost. Where the track hairpins left, go straight ahead through a gate and uphill to the vallum. Follow it over two

stiles and turn right on the metalled track to visit the **Roman Army Museum** and *Magnis* Roman Fort, and back to the car park.

POINTS OF INTEREST

Hadrian's Wall
Started by Emperor Hadrian around AD 122, the 73-mile (117.5-km) wall ran from the Tyne to the Solway Firth. One of the best surviving monuments of the Roman world, it separated Roman civilisation from the barbarians. For much of its length it follows the Great Whin Sill, a natural barrier.

Walltown Crags and Turret 45A
There were originally nine gaps – The Nine Nicks of Thirlwall – along this stretch of the Whin Sill, but only five remain because of quarrying.
Turret 45A was built before the rest of the wall and may have been a signal post used while the wall was being constructed.

Thirlwall Castle
Built in the 14th century to defend a gap in the wall against the Scots, Thirlwall Castle is a grim tower built of stones from the wall. Edward I is said to have stayed here on his way to fight the Scots in 1306. Legend says a dwarf guards a solid gold table somewhere in the castle.

The Vallum
The vallum (earth rampart), 10 feet (3m) wide at the bottom and 20 feet (6m) wide at the top, was constructed between 60 and 100 yards (55 to 90m) from the wall. Crossed only at the forts, it was the result of new military ideas that came in around AD 124.

Roman Army Museum
Next to the fort of *Magnis*, the museum contains Roman excavation finds, life-size displays of army equipment and models, as well as films about the harsh life of the Roman soldier.

Along Hadrian's Wall

Checklist

Leisure Information

Places of Interest

Shopping

The Performing Arts

Sports, Activities and the Outdoors

Annual Events and Customs

Leisure Information

TOURIST INFORMATION CENTRES

Corbridge
Hill Street. Tel: 01434 632815 (seasonal).
Haltwhistle
Station Railway. Tel: 01434 322002.
Hexham
Wentworth Car Park. Tel: 01434 652220.

NORTHUMBERLAND NATIONAL PARK CENTRES

Headquarters
Eastburn, South Park, Hexham. Tel: 01434 605555.
Once Brewed
Military Road, Bardon Mill, Hexham. Tel: 01434 344396 (seasonal).

NATIONAL PARK VILLAGE INFORMATION POINTS

Chollerford
Hexham Herbs, Chesters Walled Garden. Tel: 01434 681483.
Gilsland
Gilsland Post Office.
Tel: 01697 747211.

OTHER INFORMATION

Regional Tourist Information
www.visitnorthumbria.com

English Heritage
Tel: 0870 333 1181
www.english-heritage.org.uk
National Trust for Northumbria
Scots' Gap, Morpeth.
Northumberland.
Tel: 01670 774691.
www.nationaltrust.org.uk
National Trust Information Centre – Housesteads
Military Road, Haltwhistle.
Tel: 01434 344525.
Northumberland Wildlife Trust
Garden House, St Nicholas Park, Jubilee Road, Newcastle upon Tyne. Tel: 0191 284 6884.
www.wildlifetrust.org.uk/ northumberland
Northumbria Water
Abbey Road, Pity Me, Durham.
Tel: 0191 383 2222.
www.nwl.co.uk
Public Transport
Summer buses from Carlisle and from Hexham serve the major sites along Hadrian's Wall, linking with bus and rail services from Newcastle, Carlisle and Alston. Limited winter service. Full details are available from Tourist Information Centres.

ORDNANCE SURVEY MAPS

Landranger 1:50,000 Sheet numbers 86, 87.

Outdoor Leisure 42 (Hadrian's Wall) 1:25:000.

Places of Interest

There will be an admission charge at the following places of interest unless otherwise stated.
Aydon Castle
Corbridge. Tel: 01434 632450.
Open Apr–Oct, daily.
Border History Museum
The Old Gaol, Hallgate, Hexham. Tel: 01434 652349.
Open Easter–Oct, daily; certain days in winter.
Carrawburgh (Mithraic Temple)
On the B6315. Open any reasonable time. Free.
Chesters Bridge Abutment
Chollerford, Humshaugh. Open any reasonable time. Free.
Chesters Roman Fort and Museum
Chollerford. Tel: 01434 681379. Open Apr–Oct, daily; Nov–Mar certain days.
Corbridge Gallery
Tourist Information Centre, Hill Street. Tel: 01434 632815.
Open Easter–Oct, daily.
Corbridge Roman Site
Tel: 01434 632349. Open Apr–Oct daily; Nov–Mar most days.

Moot Hall and Gallery
Market Place, Hexham. Tel:
01434 652351. Open all year,
certain days.
Roman Wall (Housesteads Fort and Museum)
Haydon Mill. Tel: 01434
344363. Open all year daily,
except Christmas and New Year.
Vindolanda (Chesterholm)
Bardon Mill. Tel: 01434 344277.
Open mid Feb to mid-Nov daily;
phone for winter opening.
Walltown Crags and Turret
Open any reasonable time. Free

SPECIAL INTEREST FOR CHILDREN

The following places may be of
interest to visitors with children.
Unless otherwise stated there
will be an admission charge.
Border History Museum
The Old Gaol, Hallgate,
Hexham. Tel: 01434 652349.
Open Easter–Oct, daily;
Nov–Mar certain days.
Hadrian's Wall
Many milecastles, turrets and
sections of wall are freely open.
They include Brunton Turret,
near Low Brunton;
Sewingshields Milecastle, 1 mile
(1.6km) east of Housesteads,
and Milecastle 42 near
Cawfields, 2 miles (3.2km) north
of Haltwhistle.
Roman Army Museum (Carvoran)
Greenhead. Tel: 01697 747485.
Exciting museum, with a large-
scale model of the fort, push-
button displays, full-size figures
showing uniform, armour and
weapons of legionnaires. Open
mid-Feb to mid-Nov, daily.

Shopping

Haltwhistle
Market, Thu.
Hexham
Main shopping area: The
Shambles. Market, Tue.

LOCAL SPECIALITIES

Crafts
Corbridge Gallery, Corbridge
Tourist Information Centre, Hill
Street, Corbridge.
Tel: 01434 632815. Open
Easter–Oct.

Herbs
Hexham Herbs, The Chesters
Walled Garden, Chollerford.
Tel: 01434 681483.
Pottery
Bardon Mill Pottery, Bardon Mill.
Tel: 01434 344245. Large salt-
glazed pots.
The Potting Shed, 1–3
Broadgate, Hexham. Tel: 01434
606811. Terracotta pots for
house and garden.
Quilting
Fingers and Thumbs Craft,
Fellside House, 80 New Ridley
Road, Stocksfield. Tel: 01661
843608. Open by arrangement.

The Performing Arts

Hexham
The Queen's Hall Arts Centre,
Beaumont Street, Hexham.
Tel: 01434 652477.

Sports, Activities and the Outdoors

ANGLING

Contact Tourist Information
Centres and local fishing tackle
shops.

COUNTRY PARKS

Tyne Green Country Park,
Hexham.

CYCLE HIRE

Hexham
The Bike Shop, 16 St Mary's
Chare. tel: 01434 601032.

GOLF COURSES

Corbridge
Matfen Hall. Tel: 01661 886500.

Hexham
Hexham Golf Club. Tel: 01434
602057. Tynedale Golf Course.
Tel: 01434 608154.
Slaley
Slaley Hall Golf Resort. Tel:
01434 673350.
Stocksfield
Stocksfield Golf Club, New
Ridley Road. Tel: 01661 843041.

HORSE-RACING

Hexham Race Course.
Tel: 01434 606881.

HORSE-RIDING

Dipton Mill
Plover Hill Riding School,
Burnside. Tel: 01434 607196.
Haydon Bridge
Cragside Pony Trekking Centre,
Langley Road. Tel: 01434
684761.

Annual Events and Customs

Corbridge
Northumberland County Show,
mid-May.
Hexham
Abbey Festival, mid-September.
Jazz Festival, early June.

Slaley
Slaley Show, mid-August.
Twice Brewed
Roman Wall Show, early July.

*Looking out across the blue
waters of Derwent Reservoir*

Cities and Saints

The cities of Newcastle, Durham and Sunderland, at the heart of southeastern Northumbria, each have a distinctive character and history. The bones of St Cuthbert were the foundation of Durham's greatness, and other holy men – among them the Venerable Bede and St Godric – carried out their ministry here. Newcastle upon Tyne is a vibrant and friendly place with plenty of character, its active nightlife sitting comfortably alongside the many fine museums and galleries. This area is also the industrial centre of the north – still active, though altered from the days of mining and shipbuilding. And even in the clamour of the cities, fine countryside is always near by.

THE QUARRY GARDEN

If Belsay Hall is austere, even chaste, the Quarry Garden is romantic and voluptuous. Created when the stone was dug for the new Hall, it has secret, winding chasms in the sandstone, and leaf-strewn paths overhung with exotic trees and planted with rampant flowers and shrubs. Laid out by Sir Charles Monck, it is said to be based on gardens in Syracuse. Monck's grandson, Sir Arthur Middleton, carried on the plans, and developed the planting elsewhere on the estate, especially on the terrace and parterre. There is a rose garden and a magnolia terrace, all backed by woodland, glowing with rhododendrons in early summer.

BELSAY Northumberland Map ref NZ0978

The glowing yellow sandstone walls and sturdy battlements of the 14th-century tower house of the Middleton family remain almost complete. It is almost as if it were still standing ready to repel the marauding Scots who made its construction necessary in the first place. Even the Great Hall's painted wall decorations, looking just like tapestries, are well preserved.

In 1614 a manor house was added, and this was rebuilt during the 19th century. Now roofless, it was largely abandoned when Sir Charles Monck (he was originally a Middleton, but he changed his name on inheriting the property) built his startling new house a quarter of a mile (400m) away.

Belsay Hall is Greek in style and is severely plain and symmetrical, each side 100 feet (30.5m) long. The interior of Sir Charles's house – he was his own architect – is even more awe-inspiring. The central hall is two storeys high with a glazed roof, and is surrounded by columns. It is a splendid room, and perfectly proportioned, but the overall effect is rather cold.

The other rooms cannot live up to this masterpiece, although they do have fine fireplaces and good views. Only the cavernous cellars are as impressive. The Hall is now virtually unfurnished, because it was used by the military during World War II and has been unoccupied ever since.

BISHOP AUCKLAND   Co Durham Map ref NZ2028

Bishops have lived at Auckland since the 12th century, but Auckland Castle has been their main residence since Durham Castle was given to the University in 1832. The toy-like 18th-century gatehouse is just off the market place, but it is the bishops' home and its green parkland, freely open to walkers, that draw visitors to this rather dour town.

Entrance to the castle is through a Gothic screen that frames the chapel, built in the 12th century as the Great Hall and converted by Bishop Cosin after 1661. Inside is his typical dark and sumptuous furnishing. Everything – especially the ceiling – is decorated with his badge, a diagonal cross on a diamond. Much of the rest of the castle has a prosperous 18th-century look, especially the State Rooms, including the Throne Room (Durham's bishops still acted like royalty even as late as this). After all this Anglican pomp, it is pleasant to wander in the park, with Bishop Trevor's pretty Gothic deerhouse and the mature, majestic trees.

Even more than the Saxon churches at Jarrow and Monkwearmouth, the church at Escomb, 3 miles (4.8km) northwest of Bishop Auckland, takes us back to the time of Bede. Typically tall and narrow, many of its stones come from the Roman fort at Binchester nearby, where you can visit part of the headquarters building and its hypocaust heating system. Escomb church was once rather larger; you can see the outline of demolished parts indicated in stone. But otherwise only the early Gothic lancet windows, and three larger Victorian ones, have changed its appearance since well before the Norman Conquest.

BISHOP COSIN

John Cosin was one of the most able of Durham's Bishops. A Norwich man, born in 1595, he graduated from Cambridge and cared for the Bishop of Lichfield's library before becoming Chaplain to Bishop Neile of Durham. He soon became a Canon of Durham and a well-known expert on liturgy, as well as Vice-Chancellor of Cambridge University. He masterminded Charles I's coronation – his well-known hymn *Come Holy Ghost, Our Souls Inspire* was written then – and after the king's execution went into exile with the queen. At the Restoration in 1660 he was appointed Bishop of Durham. An excellent administrator as well as a man of piety, he spent time and money beautifying many churches in the county, as well as his cathedral. He died in London in January 1672, and is buried in Auckland Castle Chapel.

A gateway in the screening wall frames a view of Auckland Castle

Old wooden chairs and a rag rug frame the fireplace at Bewick's humble birthplace, Cherryburn

BEWICK'S MEMOIR
'Cherryburn House, the place of my nativity, and which for many years my eyes beheld with cherished delight, is situated on the south side of the Tyne, in the county of Northumberland, a short distance from the river. The house, stables, &c., stand on the west side of a little dean, at the foot of which runs a burn. The dean was embellished with a number of cherry and plum trees... near the House were two large ash trees growing from one root... The cornfields and pastures to the eastward were surrounded with very large oak and ash trees... It was with infinite pleasure that I long beheld the beautiful wild scenery which was there exhibited'.
– *A Memoir of Thomas Bewick*, written by himself (1828).

CHERRYBURN Northumberland Map ref NZ0762
Thomas Bewick, Britain's greatest wood-engraver and a superb naturalist, was born at Cherryburn in 1753. His countryside childhood is celebrated in the lively tailpieces he engraved for his books, especially *A General History of Quadrupeds* and the *History of British Birds*. The farmhouse, home to later Bewicks, now houses an exhibition of his life and works. You can also see the farmyard cottage where he was born, and there is a variety of farm animals around, including donkeys and pigs. On most days prints are still made from his original blocks.

CHESTER-LE-STREET Tyne & Wear Map ref NZ2751
The Romans' *Concangis* fort and their docks on the River Wear have left no trace in modern Chester-le-Street, named from its position of the Great North Road. For more than 100 years, from AD 883 to AD 995, Chester was the resting place of St Cuthbert's body, but the present church with its fine spire dates mostly from the 13th century. On the north side is The Anker's House Museum, which shows how anchorites (hermits) were walled up here; they could see the church's altar through a window inside. It was in use from 1383 until the 1530s. Best of all are the monuments in the Lumley Chapel, gathered by Lord Lumley at the end of the 16th century. Some are genuine Lumleys, from Durham Cathedral, some spurious ancestors from closed monasteries, the rest complete fakes. Some had their legs shortened to fit in.

East of Chester-le-Street, Lumley Castle, now a hotel, complete with period banquets, was built about 1390. The gatehouse has a fine display of Lumley heraldry –

James I & VI, wearied by a long tale of the Lumleys' ancestry, remarked 'I didna ken that Adam's name was Lumley'! The castle was updated by Vanbrugh in 1721; the Garter Room has splendid plasterwork, while the undercroft, now the hotel dining room, is typically masculine Vanbrugh. Near by is the ruined Lambton Castle – a picturesque 19th-century sham – and the park is now a nature reserve with pleasant walks.

Watching period drama on television – especially the novels of Catherine Cookson – will have made visitors familiar with Beamish, 4 miles (6.4km) northwest of Chester-le-Street. Set in 200 acres of beautiful countryside, the North of England Open Air Museum, has reconstructed a turn-of-the-century northern town, ideal background for clogged and shawled women haranguing their feckless men. Costumed staff welcome visitors to shops stocked with period goods, and to the pub and newspaper office, bringing Beamish vividly to life. You can take part in a lesson in the village school, worship in the Methodist Chapel, ride on a tram, catch a train or experience the hard life of the pit village – disasters in the mine sharpening the demanding daily grind. For some, the ultimate horror might be a visit to the dentist, especially after sampling the sweet factory. The Home Farm, with its traditional farm animals, used to supply Beamish Hall, once owned by the Shafto family. Amidst all the fun of Beamish, don't miss the fine statues of a shepherd and shepherdess above the doorway of the village inn.

RAILWAY FIRSTS
Causey Arch, 1 mile (1.6km) northwest of Beamish, claims to be the world's oldest railway arch. Built in 1727 by Ralph Wood, a local mason, it carried horse-drawn coal wagons 80 feet (24.4m) above a tree-lined gorge. At 105 feet (32m) long it was the largest single span bridge in the world at the time. It is now surrounded by a picnic site with displays telling its history. Near by you can catch a steam train on the Tanfield Railway, a 3-mile (4.8km) track to East Tanfield, originally opened in 1725 for horse-drawn carriages. In an area of superlatives, it also boasts Britain's oldest engine shed from 1854 – compared to the railway itself, a mere youth.

A steam rally draws enthusiasts at Chester-le-Street

TICK TOCK
The grandfather clock in the George Hotel at Piercebridge stopped the moment its owner died. This odd event reached the ears of the American songwriter Henry Clay Work, a Connecticut printer who was so adept at setting music type that he composed tunes directly in the lead blocks. The result was his song 'My Grandfather's Clock' which

'... stopp'd short – never to go again
When the old man died'.

Work was also responsible for 'Marching through Georgia' and the rather maudlin temperance song 'Come Home, Father', the emotional highlight of the melodrama 'Ten Nights in a Bar Room' when it was sung by Little Mary to her drunken papa.

STEAMING UP
Celebrating Darlington's railway heritage is a life-size locomotive, with clouds of steam emerging from its funnel. Built entirely of brick, this unusual exhibit can be seen at Morton Park beside the A66 bypass.

DARLINGTON Co Durham Map ref NZ2814

The Victorian market hall, with its proud tower, still attracts shoppers from a wide area to Darlington, for centuries an important market town. Another tower adorns Bank Top Station, a reminder that Darlington's worldwide fame comes from the first passenger railway, the Stockton and Darlington, built by George Stephenson and opened in 1825. The former North Road Station opened in 1842 and now houses Darlington Railway Centre. Its prize exhibit is Stephenson's *Locomotion No 1*, the first engine to be used on a public railway. On its maiden trip it hauled a 90-ton train, with Stephenson driving.

Fine 18th- and 19th-century houses reflect Darlington's prosperous past, and there are impressive public and commercial buildings, too – look out for Barclays Bank, in High Row. Engineering works, attracted by the railways, undertook projects throughout the world, including the Sydney Harbour Bridge.

St Cuthbert's, the 12th-century parish church, is one of the best of its date in the north. Hardly altered since Bishop le Puiset founded it about 1192, its tall spire and lancet windows make a powerful statement. The interior is solemn and well-loved.

Piercebridge, 5 miles (8km) west, is an attractive village built over a Roman camp. Dere Street crossed the River Tees here – an early bridge downstream from the village was replaced around AD 100 by another, in use until the 1200s. It is still possible to see its abutments and, it is said, oak piers when the river is very low.

George Stephenson's **Locomotion No 1** *is a highlight at Darlington Railway Centre*

DURHAM Co Durham Map ref NZ2742

Even without its finest buildings – the great cathedral and castle that dominate its skyline – Durham would be spectacular. The River Wear does a huge loop, in a deep ravine, almost to meet itself. From this superb defensive position the city grew over the centuries, down the hill and outwards, but from whichever side you approach – and especially if you arrive at the station by rail – Durham is a magnificent sight.

The three towers of Durham's Norman cathedral dominate the city

The presence of relics of St Cuthbert brought pilgrims – and prosperity – to Durham

THE PRINCE-BISHOPS

For centuries – until 1836 – the Bishops of Durham were a law unto themselves. William the Conqueror created them Earls – later they became the Prince-Bishops – to protect this remote part of his kingdom. Like some German bishops, but uniquely in Britain, they held absolute power in their very extensive lands. Bishops had their own parliament, made the law, minted the coins and controlled the army. It was they, and not the king, who gave permission for the great nobles of the north to build castles, and even the king had to ask permission to enter the Palatinate. The defence of the bishopric is still symbolised by the ceremonial presentation of a fearsome knife – the 13th-century Conyers Falchion, now in the Cathedral Treasury – as a new Bishop enters the diocese for the first time at Croft on the Tees.

DOORS TO TIME

Durham choristers have the daily experience of walking through time – or at least through the early 16th-century clock in the south transept. The large face, for some reason with only 48 minutes, is supported on marbled columns and topped with a dome and pinnacle. The doors below were painted in a rather naive style to represent a church, probably in the 17th century. The sober 19th century threw the clock out, but it is now back as the jolliest piece of furniture in the cathedral.

Durham is a place for visiting on foot. Climbing from the market place up Saddler Street you immediately get the 'feel' of the place, with small Georgian houses from one of Durham's most prosperous times interspersed with small shops and university departments, for Durham has been a university city since 1832. Owengate leads into Palace Green, dominated by the huge north side of the cathedral and surrounded by fine university buildings, with the castle to your right.

It was in Durham that St Cuthbert's bones ended their century-long journey from Holy Island in AD 995, but the present cathedral building, with its three massive towers, dates from 1093. Enter by the north door with its fearsome sanctuary ring, a 12th-century door-knocker (a replica – see the original in the Treasury).

The effect of the interior is of enormous strength. Huge columns, alternate ones incised with bold geometric patterns – spirals, zigzags and diamonds – hold up the earliest Gothic roof anywhere. Not far from the font, with its riotous canopy given in 1663 by Bishop Cosin, a black stone line in the floor shows how far women were allowed into the monastic church. The east wall is dominated by a rose window, and below it is the Neville Screen, of creamy stone. Beyond is the 13th-century Chapel of the Nine Altars, with its tall lancet windows, overlooked by St Cuthbert's tomb which has just a simple stone slab. In the choir, the Bishop's throne is the highest in Britain.

When the monks tried to build a Lady Chapel near Cuthbert's tomb, the misogynist saint is said to have supernaturally interfered with the work, so it was abandoned. Instead, in about 1170, they built a Galilee Chapel at the west end (well away from Cuthbert), perched precariously over the ravine. The tomb of the Venerable Bede is here.

Off the cloisters, don't miss the Monks' Dormitory, with its huge wooden roof, and the Treasury, full of fine silver, pre-conquest embroidery and manuscripts, and relics of St Cuthbert, including his cross and coffin. To get the classic cathedral view, go to Prebends' Bridge, reached from South Bailey.

The castle, begun in 1072, now houses University College, and its 18th-century gatehouse has a Norman core, as does the massive keep, which was rebuilt in 1840. Bishop Cosin's ornate Black Staircase leads from the medieval Great Hall to the 18th-century State Rooms and the College Chapel. The highlight of a tour of the castle, though, is the beautiful Norman gallery and the Norman chapel.

Colleges cluster in the streets around the castle and cathedral, though the university has expanded into modern buildings to the south of the city. Elsewhere, the city becomes more work-a-day, though the churches – particularly St Oswald's, near the elegant Kingsgate Bridge – are worth exploring. The Heritage Centre at St Mary-le-Bow, North Bailey, vividly tells the history of Durham, while Durham University Oriental Museum, off Elvet Hill Road, is full of wonderful Chinese porcelain and jade. The Durham Light Infantry Museum reflects the military past of the city.

A good way to see the best the city has to offer is to take this 2½-mile (4km) walk. Start in the Market Place, and from the statue of Lord Londonderry on his horse, walk along Silver Street (following the horse's nose) to descend to Framwellgate Bridge, built by Bishop Flambard in about 1128 and rebuilt after a flood in 1401. Immediately at the end of the bridge turn left down the steps by the Coach and Eight pub to the river bank, going straight ahead with the castle and cathedral across the river. Go behind the riverside buildings to Prebends' Bridge, begun in 1772 with funds from the Canons (or Prebendaries) of the cathedral. Do not cross the bridge, but continue alongside the river. On the opposite bank is the Count's House.

Follow the riverside path until it ascends into St Oswald's churchyard. Turn left into Church Street and at the end of the buildings, go left over the modern Kingsgate Bridge, then up the steps at the end and into

THE DIMINUTIVE COUNT
Count Boruwlaski, only 39 inches (1m) tall, was a talented musician and wit, much in demand amongst Durham society during the time that he lived in the city – which was from 1820 until his death in 1837 at the age of 98. The Count's House, which can be seen from the riverside near Prebends' Bridge, is actually a small Greek-style temple that the Count had in his garden.

It is delightful to explore on foot the steep, narrow streets and interesting corners of the city

Sunrise over Durham

POETIC SAINT

A pirate in his youth, the hermit St Godric lived a very simple life at Finchale (rhymes with 'wrinkle') from about 1115, alternating long hours of prayer with growing vegetables and talking to visitors, who included Abbot Ailred of Rievaulx and successive Bishops of Durham. Described as a small, agile man with 'a broad forehead, sparkling grey eyes and bushy eyebrows, an oval face, long nose and a thick beard', he died at the age of 105 in 1170. He wrote the earliest surviving verses in recognisable English and set them to still-existing music. Finchale is 3 miles (4.8km) northeast of Durham.

Bow Lane. At the top, turn left along North Bailey (if the cathedral is closed, turn right here and take the first left on to Palace Green). After about 100 yards (91.4m) go right through the 16th-century archway into the delightfully informal little square called The College. Follow the wall on the right and turn right at its end to go through a tunnel into the cathedral cloister. Go left and then right, around the cloister and into the cathedral.

Leave the cathedral by the south door and keep ahead towards the castle. At the end of the first building go left, signed Museum of Archaeology, past the house of J M Falkner, author of *Moonfleet* and *The Lost Stradivarius* who lived here in retirement and was Honorary Librarian of the cathedral. He died in 1932 and there is a plaque in his memory in the cloister. Continue down to a crossing path, turn left and follow the main path downhill to the east end of Prebends' Bridge.

Turn sharp right along the riverbank, past the Museum of Archaeology and up the steps on to Silver Street. Turn right and after a few yards take another right turn through a narrow opening into Moatside Lane. Follow the passage to emerge in Saddler Street. Turn left to the Market Place.

GATESHEAD   Tyne and Wear Map ref NZ2562
Anthony Gormley's huge steel figure of The Angel of the North stands on the edge of Gateshead (junction of the A1 and A167). It symbolises the resurgence of the town, which was long dominated by its northern neighbour, Newcastle. The other herald of regeneration is the Millennium Bridge, with its 'blinking eye' mechanism that tilts to let ships beneath it. Opened in 2001, the bridge gives pedestrians and cyclists easy passage between the Newcastle Quayside (see page 91), and the redeveloped Gateshead Quays. Dominating the south bank is the Baltic Centre for Contemporary Art developed in a former flour mill, and housing art

A WORLD OF SHOPPING
A magnet for shoppers, the MetroCentre in Gateshead is Europe's largest out-of-town shopping complex and has set the style for others throughout the UK. Designed as a leisure experience, with themed areas like the Roman Forum, Mediterranean Village and Garden Court, it offers a complete day out – including an eleven-screen cinema, a bowling alley and MetroLand, a full-scale indoor theme park. It is surrounded by 12,000 parking spaces and has its own railway station. Coach tours from far and wide make it the object of an outing. Go on Sunday and you can combine God and Mammon in a religious service conducted by MetroCentre's Chaplain.

galleries, restaurants, performance spaces, a cinema and library. Elsewhere in Gateshead is the huge Metro Centre – far more than just a shopper's paradise – and the Gateshead International Stadium. The 300-acre Derwent Walk Country Park enfolds woodland and water-meadows, while at Bill Quay Community Farm you can admire Gloucester Old Spot and Saddleback pigs, Longhorn cattle and Jacob sheep.

GIBSIDE   Tyne and Wear Map ref NZ1758
The Gibside estate was laid out by George Bowes, ancestor of Her Majesty Queen Elizabeth, The Queen Mother. The great house and most of the buildings are in ruins, but the chapel, framed by an avenue of Turkey oaks, is carefully tended by the National Trust. Designed by Paine in 1760, it was only completed in 1812. The interior is reached through a columned entrance beneath a central dome and six fine urns. It is not as ornate as Paine intended – he wanted more elaborate plasterwork and statues. The three-decker pulpit, with a cover like a pagoda roof, dominates the interior, while the small altar seems to be an afterthought.

NEWCASTLE HOPPINGS

For a real taste of Geordie enjoyment, go to Town Moor in the last full week in June. Freemen of the city have the right to graze cattle on this large green space, but animals give way to the largest travelling fair in the country during 'The Hoppings'. There are stalls and rides – complete with flashing lights, raucous music and screaming girls – stretching for more than a mile, from midday (2pm on Sunday) to late into the evening. The jollifications began last century as, strangely, a temperance festival.

On Sundays Newcastle's quayside market bursts into life – John Wesley preached here in 1742

NEWCASTLE UPON TYNE   Tyne and Wear Map ref NZ2464

Queen Victoria kept the blinds down as she entered Newcastle on the royal train. She missed a place of vibrant energy, as it still remains, and one of the friendliest of northern cities. She would probably have disapproved strongly of today's rich nightlife. Her train passed, unseeing, the keep of the New Castle itself – new in 1080 and founded by the Conqueror's bastard son, Robert Curthose. It was rebuilt 100 years later during the reign of Henry II, and there are fine views of the city from the roof.

The Victorian railway builders cut ruthlessly through the castle ward, so the medieval entrance, the Black Gate, is now separated from the keep. A picturesque brick house of about 1620 perches on top of its 13th-century lower floors.The railway goes to Central Station, a masterpiece of Newcastle architect John Dobson. The huge curved train shed, supported by slender iron columns, was much imitated. From here you can connect with the Metro System, the most convenient way of getting around Newcastle. The hub of the system is Monument Station, just by the column to Earl Grey, the 19th-century Parliamentary Reformer.

To the west is the modern Eldon Square Shopping Centre, while to the south is one of the best streets in Europe. Grey Street, lined with elegant, columned buildings, curves satisfyingly as it descends towards the Tyne. Near the top the lively Theatre Royal, where the Royal Shakespeare Company has an annual season, adds a punctuation mark with its portico.

Bessie Surtees House, nearer the river, is a survivor from an earlier Newcastle, and has a half-timbered front

The majestic sweep of Grey Street, remodelled around 1835

with a vast array of small-paned windows. From one of them, marked with blue glass, rich Bessie eloped with her poor lover John Scott; he rose to become Lord Chancellor Eldon.

The river near here is crossed by four of Newcastle's most famous bridges: Robert Stephenson's High Level Bridge was finished in 1849, with twin decks for trains and cars; the Swing Bridge was built 25 years later by Armstrongs and was once driven by their hydraulic engines; the semicircular Tyne Bridge is the one which immediately says 'Newcastle' to homesick Geordies all over the world. The Millennium Bridge (see page 88) leaps over the Tyne from Quayside where a famous Sunday morning market is held. It is also the departure point for boat trips on the Tyne.

Two church towers dominate this part of Newcastle. Classical All Saints – now deconsecrated – has a fine spire attached to a very unusual elliptical body. The Cathedral of St Nicholas, with its tall crown on the tower, was threatened by destruction from Scots' cannon fire during the Civil War, but the firing ceased when the Mayor filled the cathedral with Scottish prisoners.

Newcastle has more than its fair share of excellent museums. The University's Museum of Antiquities, with its fine displays of Roman artefacts, is the principal museum for Hadrian's Wall; the Hancock Museum, one of the finest natural history museum's in the country, houses geological exhibits and John Hancock's magnificent collection of birds; Newcastle Discovery tells the story of the city and its people. The Laing Art Gallery includes some stunning Victorian paintings, including several by local visionary artist John Martin.

Horseracing at High Gosforth Park, north of the city, is also popular. The Northumberland Plate meeting in June, a valuable two-mile handicap, is also known as 'The Pitmen's Derby' because on the day that it was run all the collieries used to be closed so that the miners could attend.

ARMS AND THE DENE
The wooded valley of Jesmond Dene, formed by meltwater retreating after the last Ice Age, was developed by Lord Armstrong, arms magnate and local benefactor. His house near by has been demolished, but the walks and bridges laid out for him remain in this most popular and unusual park, where swans can be seen on the pools and a waterfall tumbles over rocks. Armstrong used to allow visitors into his park twice a week, on payment of a small fee which helped a local hospital. In 1883 he presented it to Newcastle as a free public park, and it has been much loved and visited ever since.

TAKING THE PLUNGE
Segedunum Fort on the banks of the Tyne at Wallsend, east of Newcastle, was the most easterly on Hadrian's Wall. It has the only reconsructed bath house in the country, and illustrates the life of the soldiers as they guarded the Empire's frontier.

THE RIGHT LINES
The 'Father of the Railways' George Stephenson was born in 1781 at Wylam, across the Tyne from Prudhoe. His cottage, now owned by the National Trust, stood beside the Wylam Colliery waggonway. The famous locomotive *Puffing Billy* worked out of Wylam mine from 1813, and Stephenson's first engine, *Blucher*, at Killingworth Colliery the following year. Far-sighted Stephenson saw the immense possibilities of running trains with flanged wheels on iron rails, and his genius was to move railways from the confines of industry to passenger traffic, when he built the world's first passenger railway, the Stockton and Darlington. It opened amidst scenes of rejoicing – and warnings of disaster – in 1825.

A family of young coots at rest in Hardwick Hall Country Park

PRUDHOE   Northumberland Map ref NZ0962
The Scottish King William the Lion failed to take Prudhoe Castle in 1173 and 1174, defeated by the natural strength of the site, guarded by cliffs on the Tyne and a steep valley landward. Part of the keep still stands, surrounded by a curtain wall defending the inner and outer baileys. The castle is approached along a steep track, through a long barbican and into a gatehouse. Its chapel has a projecting oriel window which is said to be the country's first. A pretty 19th-century house in the Inner Ward has an exhibition on Northumbrian castles.

SEDGEFIELD   Co Durham Map ref NZ3528
'Racing from Sedgefield' conjures up images of peaceful, rural England, and though it is near Tyneside and Teesside, the town is just that. The racecourse is on its southwestern edge and has gained a reputation for its relaxed, warm and friendly atmosphere. At the heart of the village the church, with a grand 15th-century tower, is surrounded by tall trees and old gravestones, Georgian houses and pantiled cottages. Inside is woodwork – hearty Gothic pinnacles and luscious carving – given by Bishop Cosin's son-in law, who was rector here from 1667 and later became Dean of Durham.

An archway by the Hardwick Arms leads to Hardwick Hall Country Park. Its first owner spent so much on the garden buildings that he couldn't afford to build a house, but now most of them are in ruins, or have vanished altogether. The gateway was always a ruin, though, because it was deliberately built as such. Now the park is open for birdwatching, pond-dipping, picnicking or just strolling along the board-walk nature trail through Fen Carr.

SOUTH SHIELDS Tyne and Wear Map ref NZ3666
Signs say 'Welcome to Catherine Cookson Country', and
the South Shields area has been put on the map by the
popular author. Visitors can follow the Cookson Trail
around South Shields and visit a reconstruction of her
childhood home in the museum. Modern South Shields
has an air of maritime prosperity, with its wonderful
position at the river mouth and fine beaches. South of
the town the distinctive 76-foot (23.2-m) red and white
tower of the Souter Light, with its huge fog horn, is open
to the public.

The Romans built South Shields' *Arbeia* fort as a supply
base for the Roman army's campaign against Scotland.
The full-size reconstruction of the gateway shows the
grandeur Romans brought even to this remote part of
their empire. There are special Roman Days when
volunteers of the 'Cohors Quinta Gallorum' show how
3rd-century soldiers lived.

To the west is Jarrow, famous from the Crusade of
1936. Led by Jarrow's Labour MP, 'Red' Ellen Wilkinson,
malnourished and desperate workers, unemployed since
Palmer's Shipyard closed in 1933, marched to London,
stirring the nation's sympathy but no Government
action, except to cut their unemployment allowances for
the time they were on the road.

The Venerable Bede lived at Jarrow monastery from
AD 682, when he was 12, and wrote his *Ecclesiastical
History* here in AD 731. Incredibly, the church he knew –
dedicated in April AD 685, as we know from its
dedication stone – still survives and its nave has become
the chancel of the present building. The ruins to the
south of the church are from a later Benedictine
monastery. Across the park, the Bede's World Museum
contains finds from the site and is developing
reconstructions of Anglo-Saxon timber buildings.

*The red-and-white Souter
Lighthouse, now in the care
of the National Trust, was
opened in 1871*

'WOR KATE'
Fame and fortune would have
seemed unlikely when Katie
McMullen shared a two-
roomed flat in Tyne Dock with
her grandparents and her 'big
sister' – actually her own
unmarried mother. She
suffered from a rare blood
disease as a child, the cause of
deteriorating health in later
life, and left school at 14 to be
a laundry checker in the
workhouse. Moving south,
she saved from her laundry
manageress's wages, bought
a Sussex boarding house and
married one of her lodgers,
Tom Cookson. Years scarred
by illness and miscarriage
were the background for a
literary career that developed
spectacularly after her first
book was published in 1950.
Now read by millions, her
books are full of both tragedy
and humour, brutality and
compassion. She became
Dame Catherine Cookson in
1993, and died in 1998.

ADDED LUSTRE

Sunderland produced pottery in at least 16 factories from the early 18th century. Much of it was the famous Sunderland lustreware, decorated with iridescent glaze and black transfer prints. The most common colour is a pinky-purple, produced by adding minute quantities of gold to the glaze, although a pale copper colour and silver were also made. The thin film of lustre glaze was then splashed with drops of oil, which made the characteristic splodges. The lustre surrounded commemorative verses or inscriptions, pictures of ships in full sail or, often, a picture of Sunderland's Wearmouth Bridge. Typical products were wall plaques, jugs and joke mugs with frogs inside them.

ROKER'S BEST

The pleasant Sunderland suburb of Roker has the best Edwardian church in the country – St Andrews. Often called 'the Cathedral of the Arts and Crafts Movement', it is a massive grey building with a huge tower providing a landmark for ships. Inside it is like an upturned boat, with sweeping stone arches, and is full of wonderful things, including a tapestry by Burne-Jones behind the altar and glowing stained glass by Henry Payne. Look out, too, for the lectern with mother-of-pearl decoration and the font with its carving of vines.

A lustreware mug at the Sunderland Museum celebrates the cast-iron Wearmouth Bridge (since replaced), designed by activist Thomas Paine

SUNDERLAND   Tyne and Wear Map ref NZ3957

The city of Sunderland was once a small port surrounded by larger and better-established villages, including Bishopwearmouth and Monkwearmouth. Coal transportation and shipbuilding caused its spectacular growth in the 18th and 19th centuries, and though the shipyards no longer cluster around the mouth of the Wear, Sunderland is a bright young city. In warm weather crowds flock to the sands of Roker and Seaburn, north of the river; among varied winter entertainments is the famous pantomime at Sunderland's Empire Theatre, an Edwardian confection opened by Vesta Tilley in 1907.

A lively and interesting selection of museums can be found in and around the city. Stained glass was first made in Britain at Monkwearmouth, and Sunderland's National Glass Centre celebrates the myriad uses of glass today. It is on the Glass Trail, which takes visitors to see glassblowing and gives them the chance to buy glassware at factory prices. At the museum in Borough Road, Sunderland Lustreware pottery is on display. At Ryhope, south of Sunderland, the Engine Museum is housed in Victorian buildings reminiscent of an Oxford college chapel; the huge pumping engines of 1869, usually in steam on Bank Holidays, are an awesome sight. Across the river is the North East Aircraft Museum. Not too far away, Hylton Castle, built around 1400, has fine battlements and a resident ghost. Modern arts and crafts are shown at the Reg Vardy Arts Foundation Gallery at Sunderland University, and at the Northern Centre for

Contemporary Art. From the north end of the Wearmouth Bridge it is but a short walk to the Greek-style Monkwearmouth Station Museum, built in 1848 and preserved as it was at the turn of the century. Travel and transport in the early 1900s are recorded here, with a look behind the scenes of the booking offices and guard's van.

The Venerable Bede was born in Wearmouth in AD 673 and when he was seven entered the new monastery (hence Monkwearmouth) founded by St Benedict Biscop in AD 674. Parts of his church still survive – the lower part of the tower and part of the tall, narrow nave is 7th century, the rest of the tower is 9th century, the chancel from the 1300s and the north aisle from 1874. A small museum near by has Saxon sculpture.

TYNEMOUTH Tyne and Wear Map ref NZ3669

People crossing the North Sea on their way to the ferry terminal at North Shields get a fine view of the headland at Tynemouth, with its priory and castle guarding the entrance to the Tyne. Traces of an Iron-Age fort, later used by Romans, and a monastery from Bede's time have been found here, and it was here that St Oswin was buried after his murder in AD 651. The Danes sacked the earlier priory, and it was refounded when Oswin's bones were rediscovered in 1065. Most of what we see today dates from the end of the 12th century, although the Percy Chapel which huddles beneath it is 200 years later. The graveyard adds to its romantic setting, but the great castle gateway, occupied as part of the priory for most of its life, is grimmer.

To the south stands Tynemouth's other landmark, the gargantuan statue of Admiral Collingwood, second-in-command to Nelson at Trafalgar. Four guns from his flagship, *Royal Sovereign*, are set on the steps leading to

With nearby Roker, the beach at Seaburn provides Sunderland with its very own resort

PLAYING THE FOOL
Sir Francis Delaval was the most colourful of the family that built Seaton Delaval Hall (see page 96). He was a friend of the actor David Garrick, and himself played Othello at the Theatre Royal in Drury Lane, when his performance attracted such attention that the House of Commons adjourned early so that Members could go to watch. He made Seaton Delaval 'a fairyland of light, music and beauty', but also a place where his friends were victims of his practical jokes. They would suddenly discover, while undressing, that what they thought were solid walls in their chamber would vanish, leaving them in full public view in their nether garments. Even more alarming was his tendency to lower their beds into baths of cold water as they slept!

A novel use for a washed-up skiff at Whitley Bay

STARS AND STRIPES
The distinctive shield of the Washingtons of Washington Old Hall might have influenced one of the world's most famous flags. It shows two red stripes on a silver background, with three red stars above them. This shield is carved on the gatehouse at Hylton Castle in Sunderland and appears in other places – though, oddly, not at Washington. Despite doubters who say that the American Stars and Stripes was not derived from Washington's family arms, it is interesting to think that the Old Hall could have a direct link with the first flag unfurled on the moon.

his 23-foot (7-m) figure. Around the headland and beyond Sharpness Point is Long Sands, a fine stretch of beach. Whitley Bay is one of the northeast coast's most popular resorts, with excellent sands and Spanish City, an amusement centre that has been entertaining patrons for more than 80 years in its arcades, cafés and shops. The whole complex is now a listed building. St Mary's Island, a little way north and accessible by causeway at low tide, has pantiled cottages and a 125-foot (38m) lighthouse, now an information centre.

Inland from Seaton Sluice, north of Whitley Bay, is Vanbrugh's masterpiece, Seaton Delaval Hall. He had already built Castle Howard and Blenheim Palace, and, combining this experience with his knowledge of stage scenery as a playwright, made the house incredibly dramatic. Both the north and south fronts are monumental, with tall columns, a high central gable and turrets at each side. A fire in 1822 destroyed most of the interior, and the rooms on display today still show marks of the blaze, but the stables in the east wing escaped the fire and are as Vanbrugh left them, each stall with its horse's name emblazoned in it and with classical niches to hold the hay.

WASHINGTON Tyne and Wear Map ref NZ3155
American visitors to England's Washington will not find a city like their own capital but a New Town, based on 16 village centres, half of them completely new. Most visitors, however, will make for Washington Old Hall (National Trust), the home of George Washington's ancestors – even though most of the present building dates from around ten years after the de Wessyngtons sold up in 1613. The house is furnished in 17th-century style, with polished oak furniture, pewter plates, and some fine Jacobean panelling. There is, of course, a bust of George Washington, and a family tree that traces his ancestry to King John. Celebrations here perpetuate the American connection by marking Washington's Birthday

in February, Independence Day on 4th July and Thanksgiving in the autumn.

Coal from Washington's mines was carried to the River Tyne along the Bowes Railway, now preserved at Springwell Village. The world's only standard-gauge rope-hauled railway, it was begun by George Stephenson in 1826. You can take a ride on a steam-hauled train, follow a historical trail and visit a fascinating exhibition.

The Wildfowl and Wetlands Trust, east of Washington, was founded by Sir Peter Scott. Its 100 acres of parkland are home to flamingos, swans, geese and ducks, as well as to flocks of migrating waders and wildfowl. Some of the birds are tame enough to take food from your hand. Hides let you see the shyer species and picture windows in the Visitor Centre give views in bad weather. Man-made airborne attractions can be seen each July at the two-day Sunderland International Kite Festival held in Washington, along with street theatre, music and activities for children. This lively and colourful event, the biggest of its kind in the country, attracts kite-makers and flyers from around the world.

Dominating the landscape from its hilltop southeast of Washington is the Penshaw Monument, a soot-blackened half-size replica of the Temple of Theseus in Athens. It was built by local subscription as a tribute to the 1st Earl of Durham, 'Radical Jack' Lambton, a great local benefactor and the first Governor of Canada. Near by is another example of historical copying – the Victoria Viaduct, which is a replica of the Roman bridge at Alcantara in Spain.

THE WORM AND THE WITCH

'Whisht! Lads, haad yor gobs,
An' aa'll tell ye aboot the Warm'.

The famous Lambton Worm was hooked out of the Wear as a tiny wriggler by John Lambton, who threw it into a well and went off to the Crusades. In his absence it grew enormous and terrorised the neighbourhood, becoming so huge it 'lapped he's tail ten times roond Penshaw Hill'.

On his return Lambton tried to kill it by cutting it in two, but the halves just rejoined. The local witch told him to cover his armour with razors and fight in water. The cost of her advice was a promise to kill the first living creature he saw when the Worm was dead. Winding itself around his body, the Worm was cut into many pieces, which were carried away by the river. Lambton's plan to have a dog released at the moment of victory failed when his father came rushing triumphantly to him. Lambton refused to kill the old man, bringing a curse on the family that no male Lambton should die in his bed for nine generations – and none did.

The Penshaw Monument stands moodily over fields near Washington

Cities and Saints

Leisure Information

Places of Interest

Shopping

The Performing Arts

Sports, Activities and the Outdoors

Annual Events and Customs

Leisure Information

TOURIST INFORMATION CENTRES

Bishop Auckland
Town Hall, Market Place. Tel: 01388 604922.
Darlington
13 Horsemarket. Tel: 01325 388666.
Durham
Market Place. Tel: 0191 384 3720.
Gateshead
Central Library, Prince Consort Road. Tel: 0191 477 3478. MetroCentre Tel: 0191 460 6345.
Gateshead Quays Visitor Centre
Personal callers only.
Newcastle upon Tyne
132 Grainger Street. Tel: 0191 277 8000. Central Station. Tel: 0191 277 8000.
North Shields
Royal Quays Shopping Centre. Tel: 0191 200 5895.
South Shields
Sea Rd. Tel: 0191 455 7411. Ocean Rd. Tel: 0191 454 6612.
Sunderland
50 Fawcett Street. Tel: 0191 553 2001.
Whitley Bay
Park Road. Tel: 0191 200 8535.

OTHER INFORMATION

Durham Wildlife Trust
Rainton Meadows, Chilton Moor, Houghton-le-Spring. Tel: 0191 584 3112.
www.wildlifetrust,org.uk/durham
Regional Tourist Information
www.visitnorthumbria.com
English Heritage
Tel: 0870 333 1181
www.english-heritage.org.uk
National Trust for Northumbria
Scots' Gap, Morpeth. Tel: 01670 774691.
www.nationaltrust.org.uk
Northumberland Wildlife Trust
Tel: 0191 284 6884.
www.wildlifetrust.org.uk/northumberland
Northumbria Water
Abbey Road, Pity Me, Durham. Tel: 0191 383 2222.
www.nwl.co.uk

ORDNANCE SURVEY MAPS

Landranger 1:50,000 Sheets 81, 87, 88, 92, 93

Places of Interest

There will be an admission charge at the following places of interest unless otherwise stated.

The Anker's House Museum
Church Chare, Chester-le-Street. Tel: 0191 388 3295. Open Apr–Oct, most days. Free.
Arbeia **Roman Fort**
Baring Street, South Shields. Tel: 0191 456 1369. Open all year, most days. Free.
Auckland Castle
Bishop Auckland. Tel: 01388 601627. Open May to mid-Sep, certain days.
Bede's World
Church Bank, Jarrow. Tel: 0191 489 2106. Open all year, most days.
Belsay Hall
Tel: 01661 881636. Open all year, daily.
Bessie Surtees House
41–44 Sandhill, Newcastle upon Tyne. Tel: 0191 261 1585. Open all year, weekdays.
Binchester Roman Fort
Bishop Auckland. Tel: 01388 663089. Open Easter, May–Sep, daily.
Bowes Railway Centre
Springwell Village, Gateshead. Tel: 0191 416 1847. Open summer Sundays.
Cherryburn: Thomas Bewick Birthplace Museum
Station Bank, Mickley, Stocksfield. Tel: 01661 843276. Open Apr–Oct Thu–Mon.

Darlington Railway Centre
North Road Station. Tel: 01325 460532. Open all year, most days. Closed Jan.

Durham Castle
Palace Green. Tel: 0191 374 3863 for details of guided tours.

Durham Light Infantry Museum and Durham Art Gallery
Aykley Heads. Tel: 0191 384 2214. Open all year, daily.

Finchale Priory
Durham. Tel: 0191 386 3828. Open Apr–Oct, daily.

Gibside Park and Chapel
Rowlands Gill. Tel: 01207 542255. Open Apr–Oct, most days.

Heritage Centre
St Mary le Bow, North Bailey, Durham. Tel: 0191 384 5589. Open mid Apr–Sep, most days.

Monkwearmouth Station
North Bridge Street, Sunderland. Tel: 0191 567 7075. Open all year, most days. Free.

Museum of Antiquities
The University, Newcastle upon Tyne. Tel: 0191 222 7849. Open all year, most days. Free.

National Glass Centre
Liberty Way, Sunderland. Tel: 0191 515 5555. Open daily except 25 Dec and 1 Jan.

Newcastle Discovery
Blandford Square. Tel: 0191 232 6789. Open all year, daily. Free.

North East Aircraft Museum
Old Washington Road, Sunderland. Tel: 0191 519 0662. Open all year, daily.

North of England Open-Air Museum
Beamish. Tel: 01207 231811. Open Apr–Oct, daily; Nov–Mar, certain days.

Oriental Museum
Durham University, Elvet Hill. Tel: 0191 374 7911. Open all year, daily.

Prudhoe Castle
Prudhoe. Tel: 01661 833459. Open Apr–Oct daily.

Ryhope Engines Museum
Sunderland. Tel: 0191 516 0212. Open Easter–Dec, Sun; in steam occasionally.

St Mary's Lighthouse
Whitley Bay. Tel: 0191 200 8650. Open times vary. Check tides or telephone first.

Seaton Delaval Hall
Seaton Sluice, Whitley Bay. Open BH Mons May and Aug; Jun–Sep, Wed and Sun pm.

Segedunum
Wallsend. Tel: 0191 295 5757. Open daily.

Tanfield Railway
Sunniside, Gateshead. Tel: 0191 388 7545. Open all year daily. Free; charge for train rides.

Tynemouth Castle and Priory
Tynemouth. Tel: 0191 257 1090. Open Apr–Oct, daily; Nov–Mar, certain days.

Washington Old Hall
The Avenue, Washington. Tel: 0191 416 6879. Open Apr–Oct, Sun–Wed.

Wildfowl and Wetlands Trust
Washington. Tel: 0191 416 5454. Open all year, daily

Woodhorn Colliery Museum
Ashington. Tel: 01670 856968. Open all year, most days. Free.

SPECIAL INTEREST FOR CHILDREN

The following places may be of interest to visitors with children. Unless stated there will be an admission charge.

Bill Quay Community Farm
Hainingwood Terrace, Gateshead. Tel: 0191 438 5340. Open all year, daily. Free.

The Lambton Worm Garden and Pirates Play Area
Seaburn Centre, Whitburn Road, Sunderland. Tel: 0191 529 4872.

Lanchester Hall Hill Farm
Lanchester, Durham. Tel: 01388 730300. Open Apr–Aug, daily; Sep, Oct & Dec, Sat, Sun and school holidays.

Military Vehicle Museum
Exhibition Park Pavilion, Claremont Road, Newcastle upon Tyne. Tel: 0191 281 7222. Open Apr–Oct, daily; Nov–Mar, Sat, Sun and school holidays.

Queen Elizabeth II Country Park Railway
Queen Elizabeth II Country Park, Ashington. Narrow-gauge railway. Tel: 01670 856968. Open all year, most days.

Shopping

Bishop Auckland
Main shopping area: The Newgate Centre. Open-air market, Thu and Sat.

Chester-le-Street
Open-air market, Tue and Fri.

Darlington
Open-air market, Mon and Sat.

Durham
Open-air market, Sat. Indoor market, Mon–Sat.

Gateshead
The MetroCentre.

Newcastle upon Tyne
Main shopping area: Eldon Square. Grainger Indoor Market, daily except Sun. Quayside market Sun.

Sedgefield
Open-air market, Tue.

Sunderland
Main shopping area: Bridges Centre, open-air and covered market Mon–Sat.

Washington
Main shopping area: The Galleries.

Whitley Bay
Spanish City, market and shops.

LOCAL SPECIALITIES

Crafts
Gateway Crafts, St Nicholas Church, Market Place, Durham.

A 'big wheel' illuminates the skies of Newcastle during the city's annual fair

Food

Gregs of Gosforth, Christon Road, Gosforth, and branches throughout Tyneside. Tel: 0191 284 1411. Stottie Cake.

The Performing Arts

Darlington
The Arts Centre, Vane Terrace. Tel: 01325 486555. Civic Theatre. Tel: 01325 486555.
Newcastle upon Tyne
The Arts Centre, 67 Westgate Road. Tel: 0191 261 5618. Live Theatre, 27 Broadchare. Tel: 0191 232 1232. People's Theatre, Stephenson Road, Heaton. Tel: 0191 265 5020. Playhouse, Barras Bridge. Tel: 0191 230 5151. Theatre Royal, Grey Street. Tel: 0191 232 2061. Tyne Theatre and Opera House, Westgate Road. Tel: 0191 232 0899.
South Shields
The Customs House. Tel: 0191 454 1234.
Sunderland
Empire Theatre, High West Street. Tel: 0191 514 2517. Royalty Theatre. Tel: 0191 565 7945.
Whitley Bay
Playhouse, Marine Avenue. Tel: 0191 252 3505.

Sports, Activities and the Outdoors

BEACHES

Long Sands, Cullercoats
Good sands. Dogs restricted.
South Shields
Fine sandy beaches divided by rocky outcrops. Dogs restricted.
Sunderland
Extensive sands. Dogs restricted at Whitburn and Seaburn.
Whitley Bay
Sandy beach. Dogs restricted.

BOAT TRIPS

Durham
Prince Bishop River Cruises, Brown's Boat House, Elvet Bridge. Tel: 0191 386 9525.
Newcastle upon Tyne
River Tyne Cruises, Tyne Leisure Line. Tel: 0191 296 6740.

COUNTRY PARKS

Allensford Park, Consett.
Bolam Lake, Belsay.
Derwent Walk, Gateshead.
Lambton Castle Park, Chester-le-Street.
Queen Elizabeth II, Ashington.

CYCLING

The Consett and Sunderland Railway Path
A 20-mile (32-km) route along a former railway line.

CYCLE HIRE

Durham
Cycle Force Ltd, 29 Clearpath. Tel: 0191 384 0319.
Newcastle upon Tyne
Newcastle Cycle Centre, 11 Westmorland Road. Tel 0191 230 3022.

CRICKET

County Durham Ground, Riverside, Chester-le-Street. Tel: 0191 387 1717.
Northumberland County Club Ground, Jesmond. Tel: 0191 281 0775.

FOOTBALL

Newcastle United, St James' Park. Tel: 0191 261 1571.
Sunderland, Stadium of Light. Tel: 0191 551 551.

GOLF COURSES

Chester-le-Street
Lumley Park. Tel: 0191 388 3218.
Darlington
Haughton Grange. Tel: 01325 355324.
Durham
Durham City Golf Club, Langley Moor. Tel: 0191 378 0069.
Newcastle upon Tyne
City of Newcastle Golf Club, Three Mile Bridge. Tel: 0191 285 5481. Northumberland Golf Club, High Gosforth Park. Tel: 0191 236 2498.
South Shields
Cleadon Hills. Tel: 0191 456 0475.
Tynemouth
King Edward Road. Tel: 0191 257 4578.
Whitley Bay
Claremont Road. Tel: 0191 252 0180.

GREYHOUND RACING

Chester-le-Street
Pelaw Grange Stadium. Tel: 0191 410 2141.
Newcastle upon Tyne
Brough Park Stadium, Byker. Tel 0191 265 8011.
Sunderland
Regal Sunderland Stadium. Tel: 0191 536 7250.

HORSE-RACING

Newcastle upon Tyne
High Gosforth Park. Tel: 0191 236 2020.
Sedgefield
Tel: 01740 621925.

HORSE-RIDING

Crook
Wooley Grange, Stanley. Tel: 01388 766862.
Durham
Ivesley Equestrian Centre, Waterhouses. Tel: 0191 373 4324.

ICE SKATING

Whitley Bay Ice Rink, Hillheads Road. Tel: 0191 252 6240.

RUGBY

Newcastle Falcons, Kingston Park Tel: 0191 214 2800.

Annual Events and Customs

Ashington
Ashington Festival, October.
Durham
Durham Regatta, mid-June.
Durham Miners' Gala, early July.
Durham County Show, mid-July.
Newcastle upon Tyne
Newcastle Hoppings, late June.
Great North Run, autumn.
North Shields
Fish Quay Festival, late May.
Ovingham
Ovingham Goose Fair, mid-June.
Sunderland
Air show, early August.
Washington
Egg Rolling at Penshaw Monument, Easter.
Kite Festival, early July.
Whitley Bay
Traditional Jazz Festival, early July.

Wear and Tees

The High Pennines – 'England's Last Wilderness' – combine the majestic sweep of high moorland with deep valleys, where waterfalls thunder over sheer crags. The villages are peaceful now, but these were once thriving industrial centres. Here was the focus of Britain's lead-mining industry, and the deserted buildings and tall chimneys still punctuate the landscape as a reminder of those prosperous days.

The dramatic scenery of Weardale and Teesdale characterises this remote and captivating region, where there are wide views and secret corners, small farms and few people.

ALLENDALE Northumberland Map ref NY8355

Set 800 feet (244m) up amongst spectacular Pennine scenery, Allendale Town (as opposed to the actual dale which bears its name) is the geographical centre of Britain – a sundial on the church gives its latitude. Its pretty, irregular market place is peaceful for most of the

THE TURNCOAT CURATE

Allendale's Church of St Cuthbert had an infamous curate during the 18th century. He was Robert Patten, a supporter of the Stuarts, who became involved in the 1715 Jacobite Rebellion as chaplain to General Tom Forster. However, when he was captured, he turned King's evidence to save his own life at the expense of his friends, including the Earl of Derwentwater.

Langley Castle near Allendale Town is now a comfortable hotel

WALKS IN THE WOODS
With much of Northumbria clothed in coniferous plantation, walking in mature broad-leaved woodland is a particular pleasure. At Allen Banks, 5 miles (8km) north of Allendale Town, the River Allen runs through a heavily wooded gorge, with mature beech and oak trees clinging to the steep hillsides. This is one of the rare English places where you might just see a red squirrel, though roe deer are easier to spot. There is a suspension bridge to link the two sides of the gorge, and in Morralee Wood is a tarn.

The restored Killhope Wheel is a monument to the local lead-mining industry

year but tumultuous on New Year's Eve at the Baal Fire celebration. With its origins back in the Dark Ages, perhaps celebrating the winter solstice, the event attracts hundreds of visitors. Brave men, called 'guysers', dress up in quaint costumes and blacken their faces, carrying blazing tar barrels around the town on their heads. At midnight a huge bonfire is lit.

Langley Castle, 3 miles (4.8km) north, was built in the 14th century, ruined by Henry IV in 1405 and well-restored in 1890. It is now a hotel, but the grounds and the public rooms can be visited. The dale has not one, but two rivers – the East and West Allen – fed by many peaty burns which cascade down from the surrounding high hills.

ALLENHEADS Northumberland Map ref NY8645
The East Allen Mine was once the most important source of lead in Europe, and local landowners developed Allenheads as a model village, with a school, a library, a church and a chapel. Lead mining ended in the late 19th century, and now the village welcomes tourists – Allenheads Heritage Centre provides an excellent introduction to the area.

At the realistically named Killhope Lead Mining Centre, 2½ miles (4km) southwest of Allenheads across the County Durham boundary, the restored 1870s lead-crushing mill brings Victorian mining to life. Staff are on hand to help visitors to try their hands at the various processes, such as separating the lead ore from waste material using primitive machinery, and you can follow a discovery trail around the site to see displays of mining through the ages. The highlight of Killhope is its huge overshot waterwheel, 33 feet 8 inches (10.3m) in diameter, which has been restored to working order, and there is a visitor centre and exhibition based on the lives of the miners and their families.

BARNARD CASTLE   Co Durham Map ref NZ0516

Visitors to 'Barney' often ask 'Where's the castle?', for it is hidden from most of the town. It stands high above the Tees on the west side. Bernard (Barnard) Baliol first fortified the site, and parts of his 12th-century castle still exist, rebuilt when the Bishops of Durham and the Nevilles held it. Anne Neville married Richard III and brought the castle into his ownership. The main surviving parts are around the Inner Ward, among them the 14th-century Round Tower and the 15th-century Great Chamber – notice the boar badge of King Richard. The Tees, crossed by the County Bridge of 1569 below the castle, used to be the boundary between Yorkshire and County Durham. In the former bridge chapel, outside the jurisdiction of both the Bishop of Durham and the Archbishop of York, illegal weddings took place.

The town's wide streets – Galgate and Horse Market – were full of animals for sale in the past, and the Market

BOWES VENTURE

John Bowes was the son of the 10th Earl of Strathmore – who neglected to marry John's mother and died without legitimate children the day after his wedding to another woman. John inherited huge estates in County Durham from his mother, and became a respectable figure – MP, industrialist and collector. He married a French actress, Josephine Coffin-Chevallier. She had superb taste, he had money and organisational skills, and together they amassed the collection that became the Bowes Museum. It was always their intention to make it a public collection, but both died – Josephine in 1874 and John in 1885 – before the Museum first opened its doors in 1892.

The wonderful artefacts of the Bowes Museum are housed in an extraordinary château-style mansion

An arcaded market cross marks the main square of Barnard Castle

THE BALIOLS

Barnard Castle still bears the name of both Bernard Baliol and the castle that he built in 1125. A vast area of Teesdale came into the family via Guy de Baliol, who fought alongside William the Conqueror at Hastings in 1066. The family prospered and gained power until one John Baliol even became King of Scotland for a while, chosen from a number of contenders by Edward I of England, and enthroned on St Andrew's Day in 1292.

Place falls gently to the Market Cross, a handsome octagon of 1747. The colonnade provided shelter to the butter sellers, and the upper floor was the town hall. Notice the bullet holes in the weather vane, made in an 1804 shooting contest. Beyond the Market Cross, The Bank was once the main shopping street. Its oldest building, Blagroves House, has a tall bay window and the figure of a musician over the door. Thorngate and Bridgegate were the industrial area of the town in the 18th and 19th centuries – mill buildings and weavers' cottages, with their long upper windows, survive.

East of The Bank is The Demesnes, an area of open land which used to supply the town with water from many springs. Newgate, with the parish church, leads to Barnard Castle's greatest surprise, the Bowes Museum. Housed in a French-style château, it is one of the most remarkable private art collections in Europe, with Roman altars, porcelain, paintings by Goya and El Greco, costumes, toys, musical instruments, furniture, complete rooms from demolished buildings... don't miss the mechanical swan, which twice a day will preen itself and eat the silver fish swimming in its stream.

Egglestone Abbey, 1¼ miles (2km) southeast of Barnard Castle, was founded by Premonstratensian Canons in about 1196 – they were the White Canons, who lived a strict and severe life in the abbey. The ruins are very beautiful, with parts of the church still standing, although the Canons' living quarters have survived less well. In 1548 the Abbey, with its Canons ejected, was sold to Robert Strelley, who made part of the cloisters into an Elizabethan house – now itself a ruin.

BLANCHLAND   Northumberland Map ref NY9650

It is easier to believe that Blanchland was once home to the white-robed Premonstratensian Canons who founded the Abbey in 1165 and gave the village its name, than to several generations of workers from the nearby lead mines. For Blanchland is one of the most perfect villages in England – a cluster of stone houses, which glow golden in the sunlight, set in a deep, wooded valley among high moorland. Most of the cottages were built in the mid-18th century for Lord Crewe, Bishop of Durham, who owned the estate. When the mines had closed and the miners departed, Blanchland remained in the hands of the Crewe Trustees, undisturbed in its beauty. In the centre of the village is the L-shaped square, which may have been the monastic courtyard. It is reached from the north through the 15th-century gatehouse, complete with battlements, and from the south over the bridge – the best views of the village are from here.

Part of the church ruins were restored in the 18th century – you enter under the tower into the north transept, and turn under the crossing for the rest of the building, tall and light. Notice, on the floor, the grave slabs of abbots, carved with their mitres, and of foresters with horns. The picturesque Lord Crewe Arms next door was the Abbot's Lodge. Portraits of Lord Crewe, his wife Dorothy Forster and his niece, the other Dorothy, can be found here. The garden was the cloister of the Abbey.

A ROMANTIC HEROINE
The ghost of Dorothy Forster is said to haunt the Lord Crewe Arms in Blanchland, and to roam about the moors above. The niece of Lord Crewe, Bishop of Durham (whose wife was also Dorothy Forster), she was a real-life heroine who rode, in disguise, from here to London to rescue her brother, who was imprisoned in the Tower for his part in the Jacobite uprising under Lord Derwentwater. Her romanticised story was told in the novel *Dorothy Forster* by Sir Walter Besant, published in 1884.

Blanchland, a model village, was constructed in the 18th century, making full use of stones from the ruined abbey

Beside the Tees from Barnard Castle

One of Northumbria's crop of fascinating castles, a ruined abbey beside a beautiful stretch of the Tees and one of the country's best museums are all visited on this short walk. Mostly easy walking across fields on well-defined paths. A short stretch by the river requires care.

Time: 2 hours. Distance: 3½ miles (5.6km).
Location: 16 miles (25.7km) west of Darlington.
Start: Barnard Castle has several public car parks and some street parking. The walk begins at the Market Cross, at the end of the Market Place. (OS grid ref: NZ050163.)
OS Map:Outdoor Leisure 31 (Teesdale & Weardale) 1:25,000.
See Key to Walks on page 121.

ROUTE DIRECTIONS

From the Market Cross in the centre of **Barnard Castle**, walk up Newgate past the parish church. Cross the end of Birch Road by St Mary's Catholic Church and continue a few yards to the **Bowes Museum**.

After visiting the museum, retrace your steps towards St Mary's and take a signed track, Parson's Lonnen, between two stone walls opposite. Go through a kissing gate and follow the left hand wall as it curves. Go over a stile and ahead across the fields, called The Demesnes, to a stile. The path goes parallel with the river, crosses a concrete road and over three more stiles.

At the corner of the next field, do not go straight ahead towards the road, but through a gate in the right-hand fence and descend to join the path immediately beside the river. Go through a kissing gate and into woodland. The path here is narrow and needs care near the river, especially with children. On reaching the road, cross the bridge and turn right towards **Egglestone Abbey**.

After visiting the abbey, continue over the road bridge next to the packhorse bridge over Thorsgill Beck, and where the road bends left take a signed footpath right just after a large oak tree. Go through a squeeze stile and follow the path across a field to a stile, and then through three more fields. There are good views of the Bowes Museum and Barnard Castle School from this part of the walk. Go over a stile leading on to a metalled track.

Turn right, walk through the caravan site and at the end turn left by a waymarked fence on to a road between houses. Follow this road past a post box and by telegraph pole (ST38P), take the path right down towards a footbridge. Do not cross the river but turn left before the bridge and follow the path to the road. Turn right and walk to the traffic lights, turn right over County Bridge and then left, signed to the castle and the town centre. Follow the castle wall uphill, past the castle entrance, to Galgate. Turn right to return to Horse Market and the Market Place.

POINTS OF INTEREST

Barnard Castle
Affectionately called 'Barney', this lively town, with its two wide streets, is one of Teesdale's main centres. Approached over the 18th-century County Bridge, which once held a chapel where illicit weddings took place, the town is dominated by its 12th-century castle, once owned by Richard III. He also paid for alterations to St Mary's Church, which has good Norman work too. A cross in the churchyard commemorates the death of 143 people from Asiatic cholera in 1849. Near by is the Market Cross, paid for by local man, Thomas Breaks, in 1774. It used to be the town hall, and, from 1814, the magistrates met in its upper room. It served as the local gaol, and market traders set up their stalls under its colonnade.

Bowes Museum
What seems to be a French château was designed to house one of the best museums in the country. It opened in 1892 to house the collection formed by John and Josephine Bowes. Among its treasures are paintings by El Greco and Goya, a series of fine rooms furnished in period style

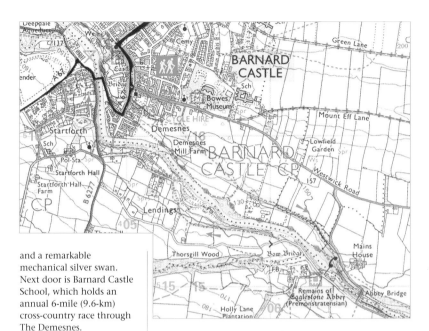

and a remarkable mechanical silver swan. Next door is Barnard Castle School, which holds an annual 6-mile (9.6-km) cross-country race through The Demesnes.

Egglestone Abbey

Much of the church, built for Premonstratensian Canons at the end of the 12th century, still stands in a beautiful spot beside the Tees. Part of the cloisters were made into a house by its Elizabethan owners.

The picturesque ruins of Egglestone Abbey stand on a well-drained hillock above the River Tees

A Perfect Village among the Hills

A circuit through moorland and along ancient tracks, with fine views of Weardale and reminders of the former lead-mining industry and Blanchland's monastic past. The moorland paths and tracks are clear, with some boggy places.

Time: 2 hours. Distance: 3½ miles (5.6km).
Location: 8 miles (12.9km) south of Hexham.
Start: Park in public car park near the former school at the north end of Blanchland. (OS grid ref: NY965505.)
OS Map: Outdoor Leisure 43 (Hadrian's Wall)
1:25,000.
See Key to Walks on page 121.

ROUTE DIRECTIONS

Turn left out of the car park in **Blanchland** and walk up the old **drove road** beside the burn. After half a mile (800m) pass the hamlet of **Shildon** on the right, and opposite the remains of a lead mine on the left, go over a stile on the right-hand side of the road, by the sign 'Blanchland Moor 1 mile'.

Follow the path left over the burn and up the steps. Go straight ahead at a crossing track, and follow the waymarked path over two wooden stiles to a stone stile with a small pond beyond it. Turn left over this stile and follow the wall to a crossing track. Turn left along the track to a gate. Go through the gate and follow the track downhill, alongside the drystone wall, bending to the left along the pine plantation. At the foot of the hill by **Pennypie House** take the track to the right, crossing a wooden footbridge over the burn.

Follow the track, cross a stile by a gate, and after half a mile (800m) meet a metalled road. Turn left, go through a gate across the road and walk down the hill to where the road bends right, go over a

Trees sprout from the stone shell of a former lead mine at Shildon

stile to the left, beside a metal gate, signed 'Blanchland ¾ mile'. Walk along the edge of the fields, passing through three gates, on to a track. Turn right and walk downhill through the farm buildings, following the track as it curves left. At the bottom of the track go through a gateway to meet the metalled road, turning right down to the car park in Blanchland.

POINTS OF INTEREST

Blanchland

The honey-coloured stone of the mainly 18th-century houses, set around two informal squares separated by an archway of the monastic gatehouse, gives Blanchland an idyllic air. Some of the buildings – notably the Lord Crewe Arms – incorporate large fragments of the former abbey buildings. Lord Crewe, Bishop of Durham – his niece was Dorothy Forster, a real-life heroine who rescued her brother from the Tower of London – rebuilt both the village and the ruined abbey church, now L-shaped and containing interesting tomb-slabs. Walk beyond the hotel and over the 18th-century bridge for the best views of the village.

Drove Road

An intricate network of drove roads, many of them still green lanes threading across the remoter parts of the area, can be found throughout Northumbria. They were used by drovers bringing livestock from the hills to the lowland markets. Some of the routes followed former Roman roads, including Dere Street, which went from York into Scotland. Other important drove roads were Clennell

Street and The Salters' Road from Alnham. This route, which leads from Blanchland to Hexham, goes over Blanchland Moor and through the area known as 'Hexhamshire'.

Shildon

The hamlet of Shildon was a centre of the important lead-mining industry from medieval times until the 19th century. There are many disused shafts and adits in the area – the walk passes one on the moorland. The ruined engine house with its tall chimney stack to the left of the road, known locally as 'Shildon Castle', was built to house a Boulton and Watt steam engine for pumping.

Pennypie House

There are two versions of how Pennypie House, set beside the Drove Road, got its name. One says it was the site of a blacksmith's shop. The smith worked for the drovers on their long journeys from Scotland to the south and he was paid for each part of the work he completed at the rate of one penny. This practice, known as 'Penny Pay', was soon corrupted into Pennypie. The other story, more straightforward, says that the enterprising householder sold pies at a penny each to the hungry drovers. You pay your money, and you take your choice.

Looking down into the green, wooded valley of Beldon Burn

The massive stone keep of Bowes Castle

DOTHEBOYS HALL
William Shaw's Academy was in a house at the west end of Bowes. The cruel and tyrannical regime under which he ran his school came to the attention of Charles Dickens, and the Academy was the original of Dotheboys Hall in *Nicholas Nickleby*. Shaw, though perhaps no worse than others who had to feed, house and educate children on a miserable allowance from their parents or guardians, was stigmatised as Whackford Squeers in the book, some of which was written at the King's Head in Barnard Castle. The inspiration for poor Smike came from the grave of 19-year-old George Ashton Taylor, a pupil of the school, which Dickens noticed in the churchyard.

BOWES   Co Durham Map ref NY9913
The A66 now bypasses the village, but it previously adhered to the line of the Roman road across Stainmore Forest, and Bowes was the site of the fort of *Lavatrae*. Only ditches mark its position, but in its northeast corner the church stands, unprepossessing outside, but with an impressive interior. It contains a stone with a long Latin inscription to the Emperor Septimius Severus, 'conqueror of Arabia and Adiabene', from the 1st cohort of the Thracian Cavalry. Bowes fort is also notable for a dedication to the Roman deity, Fortuna, which was inscribed in the bath house here, perhaps the most conducive place to muse on the part played by luck in the lives of the soldiers in this outpost of the Empire.

Bowes Castle – never more than a single keep – was begun in 1171 as one of Henry II's line of defences against Scots' raids on the border counties. It is large, solid and square, surrounded by a grassed moat, but it did not witness any major conflict. It has the same bleakness as the landscape and the village houses.

MIDDLETON-IN-TEESDALE   Co Durham Map ref NY9425
Middleton is the centre for exploring the wild landscapes of Upper Teesdale. Its stone-built houses are largely from the town's heyday as the centre of the dale's lead-mining industry. It is still possible to imagine it full of 19th-century miners. Its earlier history can be seen from the little bell-tower of 1567, like a garden summerhouse, in the corner of the churchyard, away from the Victorian church. The London Lead Mining Company's Middleton

House, with its fine clock-towered stable, is up the hill to the northwest, and the company's housing estate, Masterman Place, to the east of the town, is approached through a grand archway. In 1877 the Company Superintendent, Mr Bainbridge, gave a jolly cast-iron fountain to the town; it can be seen in Horsemarket.

Upstream from Middleton the River Tees is increasingly spectacular. The Visitor Centre at Bowlees, 3 miles (4.8km) northwest, provides an excellent introduction to the geology, archaeology, flora and wildlife of Upper Teesdale. There is a picnic site nearby, and you can walk to Gibson's Cave, where 20-foot (6m) Summerhill Force has formed a hollow in the soft rock beneath. Over the Tees is Wynch Bridge, Europe's earliest suspension bridge, originally built for miners in the 1740s. It is 70 feet (21.4m) long, and only 2 feet (61cm) wide – it was rebuilt in 1828. Just above the bridge is Low Force, a series of picturesque waterfalls. Best of all is High Force, 1½ miles (2.4km) further on and reached by a path through woods opposite the hotel – there is a good car park and a picnic area. The Tees plunges over the Great Whin Sill here, and roars into the huge gorge, at 70 feet (21.4m) the highest single-drop waterfall in England. Cauldron Snout, reached from Langdon Beck, is England's longest cascade (see Walk on page 112). There are spectacular basalt cliffs in the narrow valley below, and rare Arctic plants on the sugar limestone of Widdybank Fell.

A MORAL VEIN

In the mid-19th century, 90 per cent of all workers in Middleton-in-Teesdale were employed in the lead-mining industry – most of them working for The London Lead Mining Company. It opened its North of England headquarters here in 1815 and developed the town rapidly. The Quaker company had a paternalistic attitude, providing homes for its workers, education for their children, a library in Middleton House and encouragement for town activities like the band. It also encouraged the chapels, and insisted that every boy who wanted a job had to have a proper course of religious instruction. Foreign imports ended this beneficial despotism, and the company went bankrupt in 1905.

Bainbridge's brightly painted cast-iron fountain is a town landmark

A Rare Landscape around Cauldron Snout

The impressive Cauldron Snout waterfall, set amid the rugged and unspoiled beauty of Upper Teesdale, forms the climax of this walk. There is some walking beside a quiet road; the rest is on clear tracks and paths. There are sections of scree, with large boulders to negotiate, and some wet areas. The climb up the side of the waterfall needs special care.

Time: 4½ hours. Distance: 7½ miles (12.1km).
Location: 16½ miles (26.5km) northwest of Barnard Castle.
Start: At Cow Green Reservoir, 3 miles (4.8km) west of Langdon Beck off the B6277. (OS grid ref: NY811309.)
OS Maps: Outdoor Leisure 19 (Howgill Fells & Upper Eden Valley). 1:25,000.
Outdoor Leisure 31 (North Pennines – Teesdale & Weardale) 1:25,000.
See Key to Walks on page 121.

ROUTE DIRECTIONS

From the car park beside **Cow Green Reservoir**, walk alongside the entry road, past information boards and straight on, ignoring paths signed 'Cauldron Snout', through a former lead mining area. Pass a brick hut and later a small tarn on the left, then go over a bridge and through a gate beside a cattle grid. Continue in the same direction for another mile (1.6km), with **Widdybank Fell** to the right, through three more gates by grids. After the third grid turn right on a track signed 'Public footpath'.

Pass a second cattle grid and follow a track for a mile (1.6km) towards **Cronkley Scar**. The **Pennine Way** joins the track just before Widdy Bank Farm. Go through three gates across the farmyard and over a stone stile beside the fourth gate. Continue alongside the River Tees for

2 miles (3.2km), first on turf paths but later with some difficult scrambling over large boulders or through boggy areas (boardwalks and paved areas in places).

As the river bends right, **Falcon Clints** comes into view on the right. Follow the river round the crags to reach **Cauldron Snout** waterfall. Very carefully climb the rocks beside the fall – there are several paths, those furthest away being slightly easier – and follow the stone path towards the dam wall. At a metalled track turn right and walk beside Cow Green reservoir for 1½ miles (2.4km), passing a weather station, to a metal gate. Go through the kissing gate beside it, turn left along a track then right along a path to return to the car park.

POINTS OF INTEREST

Cow Green Reservoir
The reservoir, serving

Teesmouth industries nearly 50 miles (80km) east, was completed in 1971, amid concern from conservationists, who feared that the unique flora of Upper Teesdale, unchanged since the last Ice Age, would be destroyed. Rescued plants, and displays on natural history and geology, can be seen at Bowlees Visitor Centre near Middleton-in-Teesdale.

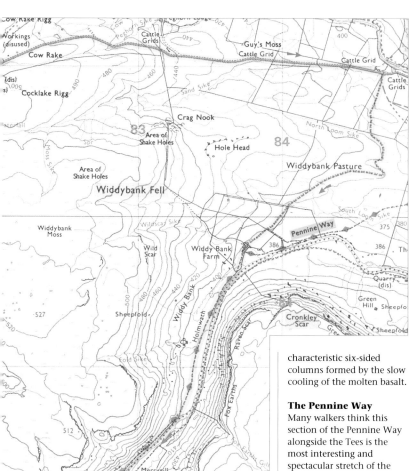

Widdybank Fell

When the Great Whin Sill was formed, the existing limestone, laid down when this part of the land was covered by sea, was changed by contact with the very hot volcanic rock into the rare sugar limestone of Widdybank Fell. On the lime-rich soils, undisturbed since the glaciers retreated, grow sub-arctic plants, including spring gentian, Teesdale violet and the unique Teesdale or bog sandwort. This area is a National Nature Reserve.

Cronkley Scar and Falcon Clints

The towering 325-foot (100-m) black rocks of Cronkley Scar are part of the Whin Sill. The summit behind rises to 1,794 feet (544m). Lower down are far older Silurian slates; a factory once produced pencils here. Falcon Clints, another Whin Sill outcrop, displays the characteristic six-sided columns formed by the slow cooling of the molten basalt.

The Pennine Way

Many walkers think this section of the Pennine Way alongside the Tees is the most interesting and spectacular stretch of the 256-mile (412-km) route. Boardwalks and resurfacing of the path indicate the fragility of the landscape and the importance of keeping to the signed routes.

Cauldron Snout

Approaching Cauldron Snout this way, it is easy to appreciate the power of the fall in its rocky chasm on the Whin Sill. Measured from the first cataract to the last, Cauldron Snout is the highest waterfall in England – it drops by 200 feet (60m), and is especially impressive after rain. The ascent beside it needs extreme care.

The high road over Harthope Moor leads to the little town of St John's Chapel

CORAL AND MARBLE
Weardale seems an unlikely place to find coral, but in the marble quarried at Frosterley, between Stanhope and Wolsingham, it can be found fossilised. Frosterley marble – it is really a form of black limestone that can be highly polished – has been used inside many churches in the North of England, usually as thin columns clustering around larger ones. There are fine examples in the Chapel of Nine Altars at Durham Cathedral and the chapel at Auckland Castle. The marble was transported to them on barges which were floated down the Wear.

ST JOHN'S CHAPEL Co Durham Map ref NY8837
St John's Chapel in Weardale can be reached by the highest classified road in England, over Harthope Moor from Teesdale. The church, overlooking the small square with its diminutive Town Hall, was rebuilt in 1752 with impressive classical columns inside. There are pleasant footpaths all around, and access across a footbridge to the Weardale Way. At Ireshopeburn, a mile (1.6km) west, is the Weardale Museum in a former Manse, with reconstructions of Dale life around 1870. Next door is the 18th-century chapel where John Wesley preached – a room in the museum is dedicated to him.

The market town of Stanhope, lower down the valley amid woodland, is known as the Capital of Weardale. By the churchyard entrance is a fossilised tree-stump, said to be 250 million years old. Rather less ancient were the entire possessions of a Bronze-Age family found in Heathery Burn Cave in 1850. Now in the British Museum, they showed early use of wheeled vehicles and horses. Another transportation method, the Heritage Line railway, is preparing to run trains on the branch line from Stanhope to Bishop Auckland. Stanhope has an open-air swimming pool, and there are stepping stones across the Tees to riverside walks. The Durham Dales Centre combines craft shops and tearoom with the Tourist Information Centre. The oldest agricultural show in England is held on the first weekend in September at Wolsingham, 6 miles (9.6km) west.

STAINDROP Co Durham Map ref NZ1220

King Canute gave the Staindrop estate to the Community of St Cuthbert in around 1031, and in 1378 Bishop Hatfield of Durham gave the village a charter to hold a weekly market. The market survived until 1858, when Barnard Castle took over.

There are long greens, narrowing towards the bridge and the church, which has substantial Saxon stonework incorporated in Norman and later work. Notice the blocked Saxon windows above the nave arches. Dominating the west end are grand memorials to members of the two great families who have owned near by Raby Castle: The Nevilles, Earls of Westmorland, get one corner, and the Vanes, Dukes of Cleveland, who were later owners, occupy the other. Ralph Neville, the 1st Earl, lies in armour between his two wives, carved in alabaster; Henry, the 5th Earl, makes do with oak, while the 1st Duke has a fine marble effigy. There is an overflow collection of Cleveland tombs in the churchyard, in a mausoleum which dates from 1850.

Raby Castle, to the north of Staindrop, may be on the site of Canute's palace – the Nevilles married into his family. It is one of the most beautifully positioned castles in the country, with nine towers and battlements overlooking the lake, and superb gardens to offset its warlike appearance. In the Middle Ages it had an immensely strong curtain wall, 30 feet (9m) high, presenting a harsh front to an unsettled land.

The castle has been well connected during its rich history – Richard III's mother, Cecily Neville, 'The Rose of Raby' was brought up here by her father, the Ist Earl. Later the 6th Earl forfeited the castle for trying to put Mary, Queen of Scots on the throne in 1596 – James I & VI seized and re-fortified it, then sold it to his Secretary of State, Henry Vane. The second Sir Henry at Raby also fell foul of the monarchy and was executed by Charles II, but the family survived and still owns the castle.

ESTATES UNSPOILED

Everywhere you go in Teesdale there are traditional lime-washed farm houses and cottages, a perfect foil for the often rugged landscape. They mostly belong to the Raby Estate, a huge tract of land north of the river, and the tenants have to renew the wash every year. South of the river, on estates owned by the Earls of Strathmore – the Bowes-Lyons – the buildings are left in their natural stone, but kept in equally good repair. It is in large part the careful custodianship of these two estates, as well as other landowners, that has kept the wilder parts of the High Pennines so unspoiled.

Moated Raby Castle enjoys a magnificent setting in an extensive deer park

Hamsterley Forest is Jorrocks country, for the 6,177-acre forest is on the former estate of the Surtees family – R S Surtees wrote the famous hunting novels about the London grocer, John Jorrocks, who became a Master of Foxhounds. The forest is open to visitors, who can walk along waymarked trails, take part in orienteering, picnic or follow the attractive Forest Drive. The Visitor Centre has displays about the woodland and its wildlife.

The Italianate stately home of Rokeby Park was sold to pay off debts just 30 years after its building; Scott's poem Rokeby, *set in this 'beautiful demesne', is dedicated to an ancestor of the new owner, John Sawrey Morritt*

Clifford's Tower and Bulmer's Tower remain from the original building, and there is still a perfect 14th-century kitchen with huge fireplaces. The cobbled inner courtyard is reached through the spectacular Neville Gateway. When the castle was restored by John Carr in the 1760s, a long tunnel was created so that carriages could drive through the Lower Hall and out under the Chapel Tower.

Carr recreated the interiors, too – his entrance hall, with its blood-red columns is particularly impressive – and from the 1840s come the stunning French-style Octagon Room, and the 130-foot (40-m) Baron's Hall. Don't miss Hiram Powers' chained and naked 'Greek Slave Girl' in white marble, which caused a sensation at the Great Exhibition of 1851. The stables are worth a visit, too, for their collection of carriages, and the splendid gardens have a number of rare trees and shrubs, including a fig tree which was planted in 1768. The castle and its gardens are surrounded by an extensive deer park.

Rokeby Park, 5 miles (8km) southwest of Raby, provides a complete contrast. It is an urbane classical house, its stone centre block contrasting with the sunny ochre wash of its wings. Designed for himself by the extravagant Sir Thomas Robinson, the house was finished in 1731. The interior decoration is superb, particularly in the central saloon, which rises to the full height of the house, and has a gilded ceiling and marble fireplaces. This is where the famous Velasquez painting, *The Rokeby Venus*, now in the National Gallery, was originally hung. Just south of the park is Greta Bridge, once a favourite romantic spot, painted by artists such as Turner and Cotman.

TEESDALE VILLAGES Co Durham

From Barnard Castle the B6277 passes through attractive landscape above the Tees and through pleasant villages.

In Lartington, where the area's largest show, the Teesdale Country Fair, is held, you can get a glimpse of Lartington Hall, an 18th-century building once the home of the Roman Catholic Maire family – their monuments are in Romaldkirk church. The Hall is not open, but the gardens can occasionally be visited.

Cotherstone is set above the river, its pretty houses following the winding road. The castle, of which virtually only the mound – known as The Hagg – remains, was built by the Fitzhughs where the River Balder joins the Tees. A minor road alongside the Balder will take you to a chain of reservoirs, where you can enjoy waymarked walks, water-skiing and fishing.

Romaldkirk is, perhaps, an even prettier village, with irregular greens, complete with traditional stocks and pump, and a large church that is full of interest. This peaceful place had a harsher past – it was sacked by King Malcolm of Scotland in 1070, and devastated by plague in 1644.

The 17th-century Eggleston Bridge crosses the Tees to Eggleston, once a lead-mining centre, though all traces of that industry have vanished. The gardens of Eggleston Hall, with their fine shrubs, mature trees and greenhouses, are open to the public, and you can buy herbs and other plants, fruit and organically-grown vegetables.

From Mickleton there is a pleasant 2-mile (3.2-km) level walk towards Middleton-in-Teesdale along the disused railway line. It starts at the former railway station off the minor road that goes south from the crossroads in the village centre.

Neatly kept houses on Cotherstone's village green

COTHERSTONE CHEESE

The traditional Cotherstone cheese is still made on a village farm, though the days are gone when it was produced by almost every farmer's wife in the area. It is a full-fat, cow's milk cheese, locally eaten when it is young – then it is mild and crumbly, rather like a softer version of Wensleydale, but with its own distinctive flavour. There is also a smoked version. You can buy it from several local outlets. It is available further afield, too, but then it is more mature, with a hard rind and a sharper, though no less attractive, taste.

Wear and Tees

Checklist

Leisure Information

Places of Interest

Shopping

Sports, Activities and the Outdoors

Annual Events and Customs

Leisure Information

TOURIST INFORMATION CENTRES

Barnard Castle
Woodleigh, Flatts Road.
Tel: 01833 690909.
Middleton-in-Teesdale
10 Market Place. Tel: 01833
641001.
Stanhope
Durham Dales Centre, Castle
Gardens. Tel: 01388 527650.

OTHER INFORMATION

**Regional Tourist
Information**
www.visitnorthumbria.com
Durham Wildlife Trust
Rainton Meadows, Chilton
Moor, Houghton-le-Spring. Tel:
0191 584 3112.
www.wildlifetrust.org.uk/
durham
English Heritage
Tel: 0870 333 1181
www.english-heritage.org.uk
**National Trust for
Northumbria**
Scots' Gap, Morpeth.
Northumberland.
Tel: 01670 774691.
www.nationaltrust.org.uk
**Northumberland Wildlife
Trust**
Garden House, St Nicholas Park,

Jubilee Road, Newcastle upon
Tyne. Tel: 0191 284 6884.
www.wildlifetrust.org.uk/
northumberland
Northumbria Water
Abbey Road, Pity Me, Durham.
Tel: 0191 383 2222.
www.nwl.co.uk

ORDNANCE SURVEY MAPS

Landranger 1:50,000 Sheets 86,
87, 88, 91, 92, 92. Outdoor
Leisure 1:25,000 Sheets 31, 43.

Places of Interest

There will be an admission
charge at the following places of
interest unless otherwise stated.
Allenheads Heritage Centre
Open all year daily. Tel: 01434
685395.
Bowes Castle
Bowes. Large stone keep,
surrounded by grassed moat.
Open any reasonable time. Free.
The Bowes Museum
Barnard Castle. Tel: 01833
690606. Open all year, daily.
Bowlees Visitor Centre
Bowlees, Middleton-in-Teesdale.
Tel: 01833 622292. Open
Apr–Oct daily; Nov–Mar,
weekends.
Castle
Barnard Castle. Tel: 01833

638212. Open Apr–Oct, daily;
Nov–Mar, most days.
Durham Dales Centre
Castle Gardens, Stanhope.
Tel: 01388 527650. Open
all year, daily. Free.
Egglestone Abbey
Barnard Castle. Open any
reasonable time. Free.
Eggleston Hall Gardens
Eggleston, Barnard Castle. Tel:
01833 650403. Open all year,
daily.
**Killhope Lead Mining
Centre**
Cowshill. Tel: 01388 537505.
Restored Victorian lead-crushing
mill with visitor centre and
exhibition. Open Apr–Oct,
daily.
Raby Castle
Staindrop. Tel: 01833 660202.
Magnificent 14th-century castle
with a deer park, lakes and
walled garden. Open Easter,
May–Sep, certain days.
Rokeby Park
Rokeby, Barnard Castle. Tel:
01833 637334. Open
May–Sep, certain days.
**Weardale Museum of High
House Chapel**
Ireshopeburn. Tel: 01388
537417. Open May–Jul and
Sep certain afternoons; Aug
daily.

SPECIAL INTEREST FOR CHILDREN

Durham Dales Centre
Castle Gardens, Stanhope. Tel: 01388 527650. Open all year, daily. Free.

Shopping

Barnard Castle
Market, Wed.

LOCAL SPECIALITIES

Cheese
Cotherstone cheese is available from several local outlets in and near Barnard Castle.

Textiles
The Weavers, Forge Cottage, Ireshopeburn. Tel: 01388 537346.

Sports, Activities and the Outdoors

ABSEILING

Middleton-in-Teesdale
Hudeway Centre, Hudeway Stacks Lane. Tel: 01833 640012.

ANGLING

For information contact local Tourist Information Centres and fishing tackle shops.

Coarse
Rivers Wear and Tees: Contact local Tourist Information Centres.
Blackton Reservoir: Tel: 01833 641121. Permits from machine at Fishing Lodge.
Cow Green Reservoir: Tel: 01833 641121. Permits from Fishing Lodge.
Derwent Reservoir: Tel: 01207 255250. Permits from machine at Fishing Lodge or shop in Edmondbyers.
Grassholme Reservoir: Tel: 01833 641121. Permits from machine at Visitor Centre by dam or from Cotherstone Post Office.
Hury Reservoir: Tel: 01833 641121. Permits from machine at Fishing Lodge or from Cotherstone Post Office.

CAVING AND CLIMBING

Middleton-in-Teesdale
Hudeway Centre, Hudeway Stacks Lane. Tel: 01833 640012.

COUNTRY PARKS

Edmundbyers Pow Hill Country Park, Derwent Reservoir.

CYCLE HIRE

Barnard Castle
Hamsterley Forest Bikes, 36B The Bank. Tel: 01833 690194.
Frosterley
Weardale Mountain Bikes, 39 Front Street.
Tel: 01388 528129.

GOLF COURSES

Allendale
Allendale Golf Club, High Studdon, Allenheads Road. Tel: 01434 683926.
Barnard Castle
Barnard Castle Golf Club, Harmire Road.
Tel: 01833 638355.

HORSE-RIDING

Barnard Castle
Offroaders, Deepdale Offroad, Smartgill Farm, Bowes Road, Barnard Castle. Tel: 01833 630802.
Hamsterley
Hamsterley Riding School.
Tel: 01388 488328.
Lartington
Raygill Riding Centre, Raygill Farm. Tel: 01833 690118.
Weardale
Alston and Killhope Riding Centre, Low Cornriggs Farm, Cowshill. Tel: 01388 537600.

ORIENTEERING

Hamsterley Forest
For information, tel: 01388 488312.

Middleton-in-Teesdale
Hudeway Centre, Hudeway Stacks Lane. Tel: 01833 640012.

WATERSPORTS

Allenheads
Allenheads Lodge. Tel: 01434 685374.
Middleton-in-Teesdale
Hudeway Centre, Hudeway Stacks Lane. Tel: 01833 640012

Annual Events and Customs

Allendale
Allendale Fair, early June. Agricultural Show, mid-August. Baal Festival, New Year's Eve.
Barnard Castle
Meet Weekend, late May.
Bowes
Agricultural Show, early September.
Eastgate
Spring Sheep Show, late May.
Eggleston
Eggleston Agricultural Show, mid September. St John's Chapel Weardale Agricultural Show, late August.
Stanhope
Agricultural Show, early September.

The checklists give details of just some of the facilities in the area covered by this guide. Further information is available from Tourist Information Centres.

Schoolchildren enjoy a spot of 'hands-on' industrial history at Killhope

Atlas and Map Symbols

THE NATIONAL GRID SYSTEM

The National Grid system covers Great Britain with an imaginary network of 100 kilometre grid squares. Each square is given a unique alphabetic reference as shown in the diagram. These squares are sub-divided into one hundred 10 kilometre squares, each numbered from 0 to 9 in an easterly (left to right) direction and northerly (upwards) direction from the bottom left corner. Each 10 km square is similarly sub-divided into one hundred 1 km squares.

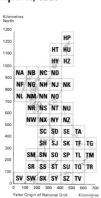

KEY TO ATLAS

MOTORWAY

(M4)	Motorway with number
Fleet	Motorway service area
	Motorway junction with and without number
3	Restricted motorway junctions
	Motorway and junction under construction

PRIMARY ROUTE

(A3)	Primary route single/dual carriageway
Grantham North	Primary route service area
BATH	Primary route destinations
	Roundabout
Y 5 Y	Distance in miles between symbols
	Narrow Primary route with passing places

A ROAD

A1123	Other A road single/dual carriageway
	Road tunnel
Toll	Toll
	Road under construction
	Roundabout

B ROAD

B2070	B road single/dual carriageway
	B road interchange junction
	B road roundabout with adjoining unclassified road
	Steep gradient
	Unclassified road single/dual carriageway
	Railway station and level crossing

KEY TO ATLAS

⛪	Abbey, cathedral or priory	– – – –	National trail
🐠	Aquarium	NT	National Trust property
♜	Castle	NTS	National Trust for Scotland property
⌒	Cave	↙	Nature reserve
♼	Country park	★	Other place of interest
🏏	County cricket ground	P+R	Park and Ride location
🐖	Farm or animal centre	⚲	Picnic site
··········	Forest drive	⚙	Steam centre
✿	Garden	🎿	Ski slope natural
⚑	Golf course	🎿	Ski slope artifical
⌂	Historic house	ⓘ	Tourist Information Centre
🐎	Horse racing	☀	Viewpoint
🏍	Motor racing	ⓥ	Visitor or heritage centre
🏛	Museum	🐾	Zoological or wildlife collection
☎	AA telephone		Forest Park
✈	Airport	····	Heritage coast
Ⓗ	Heliport		National Park (England & Wales)
⚒	Windmill		National Scenic Area (Scotland)

KEY TO TOURS

🚗	Tour start point	Buckland Abbey	Highlighted point of interest
→	Direction of tour		Featured tour
▸▸▸	Optional detour		

KEY TO WALKS

Scale 1:25,000, 2½ inches to 1 mile, 4cm to 1 km

	Start of walk	Line of walk
➡	Direction of walk	⊩•┤• Optional detour
	Buckland Abbey	Highlighted point of interest

ROADS AND PATHS

M1 or A6(M)	M1 or A6(M)	Motorway
A 31(T) or A35	A 31(T) or A35	Trunk or main road
B 3074	B 3074	Secondary road
A 35	A 35	Dual carriageway
		Road generally more than 4m wide
		Road generally less than 4m wide
		Other road, drive or track
		Path

Unfenced roads and tracks are shown by pecked lines

RAILWAYS

Multiple track	Standard gauge	Embankment
Single track		Tunnel
Narrow gauge		Road over; road under
Siding		Level crossing
Cutting		Station

PUBLIC RIGHTS OF WAY

Public rights of way may not be evident on the ground

Public paths	footpath bridleway	Byway open to all traffic
Permissive path		Road used as a public path
Permissive bridleway	Pennine Way	Named path
		National trail or recreational path

The representation on this map of any other road, track or path is no evidence of the existence of a right of way

RELIEF

50 · 285 ·	Heights determined by	Ground survey Air survey

Contours are at 5 and 10 metres vertical interval

SYMBOLS

	Place of worship	with tower	○ W. Spr Well, Spring
		with spire, minaret or dome	Gravel pit
		without such additions	Other pit or quarry
	Building		Sand pit
	Important building		
· T; A; R	Telephone: public; AA; RAC		Refuse or slag heap
--□---- pylon pole	Electricity transmission line		County Boundary (England & Wales)
△ △	Triangulation pillar		Water
	Bus or coach station		
人 人	Lighthouse; beacon		Sand; sand & shingle
⊹	Site of antiquity		National Park boundary
NT	National Trust always open		
FC	Forestry Commission		Mud

DANGER AREA

Firing and test ranges in the area
Danger!
Observe warning notices

VEGETATION

Limits of vegetation are defined by positioning of the symbols but may be delineated also by pecks or dots

⋀ ⋀	Coniferous trees	Non-coniferous trees
○ ○ ○	Orchard	Heath
⅋ ⅋	Coppice	Marsh, reeds, saltings.

TOURIST AND LEISURE INFORMATION

⋀	Camp site	PC	Public convenience
🛈	Information centre	P	Parking
i	Information centre (seasonal)	☀	Viewpoint
🚐	Caravan site	⊕	Mountain rescue post
✕	Picnic site		

Ayton

A1

A6105

B6460

Berwick-upon-Tweed

0   2   4   6   8 mls
0 2 4 6 8 10 km

B6461

orham

A698

B6354

Ancroft

nhill-
weed

B6525

B6353

*Causeway flooded
at high tide*

Holy Island

B6353

Lowick

15

A1

B6352

14

B6525

B6351

Kirknewton

Doddington

Belford

B6349

B1342

Bamburgh

Farne Islands

Seahouses

Wooler

A697

B6348

Chatton

B6348

B1341

Beadnell

THE CHEVIOT
816

B6346

17

Eglingham

B6341

B6346

B1340

Embleton

B1339

B1338

Powburn

16

B6346

B6341

A1

Longhoughton

Glanton

Alnwick

B6341

7

8

Alnmouth

A1068

B6341

Rothbury

B6345

Warkworth

Amble

Thropton

Longframlington

B6342

5 B6344

4

19

Felton

Broomhill

B6345

B1330

Red Row

8

Otterburn

Elsdon

16

Longhorsley

9

A1

Widdrington

B1337

A1068

UMBERLAND

A697

urn

A696

Ridsdale

B6342

Cambo

B6343

A197

ASHINGTON

Newbiggin-
by-the-Sea

gham

Kirkwhelpington

A192

Morpeth

A196

A189

BLYTH

A68

B6342

B6524

BEDLINGTON

A193

Colwell

Belsay

A1

Cramlington

A190

Seaton Delaval

A6079

A696

14

A192

Earsdon

WHITLEY BAY

Chollerford

Ponteland

A18

Seaton Burn

A191

Cullercoats

TYNEMOUTH

Wall

B6318

Darras
Hall

B6323

A1

A189

A19

North Shields

SOUTH SHIELDS

B6318

B6321

GOSFORTH

NEWCASTLE
UPON
TYNE

A191

Wallsend

A69

Ryton

JARROW

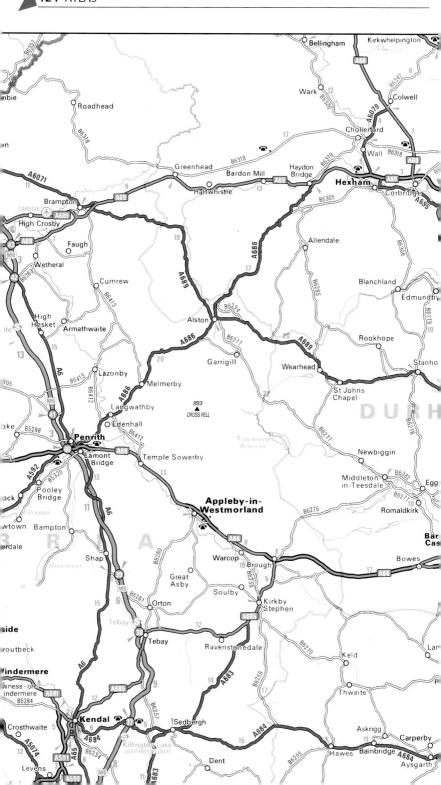

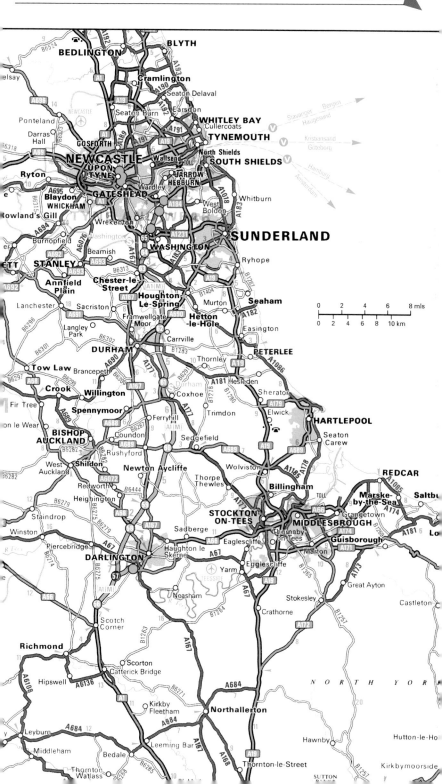

Index

Acknowledgements

The author would like to thank the patient staff at the Tourist Information Centres throughout Northumbria and all those who, knowingly or not, have helped with the preparation of this book.

The Automobile Association wishes to thank the following photographers, libraries and associations for their assistance in the preparation of this book

THE MANSELL COLLECTION LTD 7b
NATURE PHOTOGRAPHERS LTD 33 (E A Janes), 45 (P R Sterry)
TYNE & WEAR MUSEUMS 94

All remaining are held in the Association's own library (AA PHOTO LIBRARY) and were taken by C Lees with the exception of pages 3f, 6d, 8b, 11d, 15, 34 (J Beazley), 6e, 8/9, 52, 67, 117 (S & O Mathews)